T0128204

THE DE-EVOLUTION OF THE BLACK CHURCH

Rescue or Recovery

L.D. Williams

authorHOUSE®

AuthorHouse™
1663 Liberty Drive
Bloomington, IN 47403
www.authorhouse.com
Phone: 1 (800) 839-8640

Published by AuthorHouse 01/21/2017

ISBN: 978-1-5246-5793-2 (sc)
ISBN: 978-1-5246-5791-8 (hc)
ISBN: 978-1-5246-5792-5 (e)

Library of Congress Control Number: 2016921624

Print information available on the last page.

This book is printed on acid-free paper.

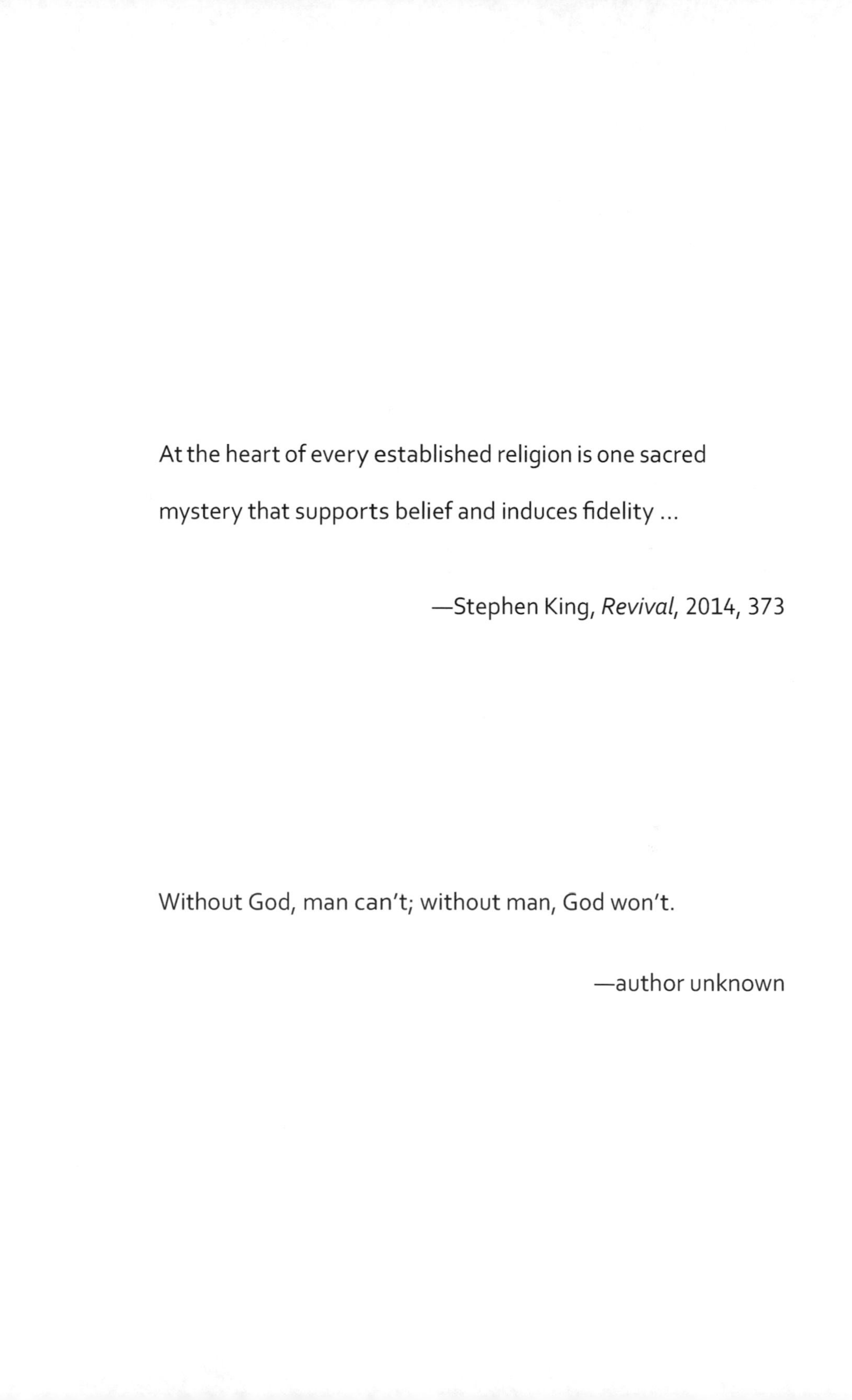

At the heart of every established religion is one sacred mystery that supports belief and induces fidelity …

—Stephen King, *Revival*, 2014, 373

Without God, man can't; without man, God won't.

—author unknown

PREFACE

On September 27, 2014, Mount Ontake erupted near Tokyo, Japan. There was no warning as the hiking area was pummeled with volcanic ash and explosive power comparable to some military exchanges. Immediately, the Red Cross and other rescue agencies attempted to save as many as they could from the volcano; however rescue efforts had to be suspended because of the winds and other treacherous elements that could not be overcome.

The mission went from one of rescue to one of recovery of the numerous victims who'd died. Many complained to their government of little or no warning of the eruptions, despite all the technological advancements to track seismic activity. The concerned public believed that had there been forewarning, the loss of lives could have been avoided.

A similar travesty could be occurring within the black church. Perhaps it is already too late.

There have been signs and wonders for years since the American

Civil Rights Movement. We as a people, and we as a nation, have observed it but sat back much like many opponents to human intervention to combat climate change have. The opponents believe that the earth will in time heal itself.

Perhaps it is time to concede that the black church is beyond rescue, died a long time ago, and now we are in a state of recovery: THE RECOVERY OF OUR EVER LOVING MINDS.

Maybe I should start at the beginning. Not the beginning but *the* beginning when my left brain began shouting at my right brain.

On February 24, 2010, I read something that opened up a new phase of self-discovery in my life. Eddie Glaude Jr., PhD, professor of religion and chair of the Center of African American Studies at Princeton University, wrote an article for the *Huffington Post* entitled "The Black Church Is Dead."[1]

Dr. Glaude, himself African American, had issued this proclamation, and the obvious question I had was whether there was any merit to Professor Glaude's statement. This obviously educated man had the courage to actually publish it and have his article posted on the internet for all to see. Was he mad? Insane? He was going to be vilified by people of color across America forever. He was going to be ostracized by the black church and demonized in his community, and he would suffer

---

1 Glaude, "The Black Church."

greatly for speaking out against God! I immediately began praying for his family and looking on the Internet to make sure there were no violent physical reprisals against him or his family.

I knew that articles would be written in response—I knew it. EUR, Black America Web, The Root, Bossip, the religious networks such as the Word Channel, TCT—these folks were about to have a jihad against Dr. Glaude.

Mine was a knee-jerk, panic-stricken reaction. Suddenly, though, I became inspired and calmed myself down and began to think logically about this. Yes, I said "logic," the bane to all religion and especially the black church. I was using my Pharisiee-tical skills as an attorney and litigation specialist to interpret exactly what the good doctor had said and prayed that I could help him help himself.

Dr. Glaude did not know it, but two years prior to the publishing of his article, I was in the throes of breaking away from the black church, organized religion and a near lifetime of grappling with the myriad theological interpretations of the Bible from various religious figures through the years. I became sick of church and being "churched".

Dr. Glaude said the black church, though. He wasn't talking about my personal affiliation with one of the churches in my community. He was speaking of the black church, that monolithic, unifying, all-encompassing force that all black people in the United States, regardless of geographic distance, socioeconomic status, education, and denomination were a part of whether they had conscious knowledge of its existence or even wanted membership in its ranks. You were automatically included in the membership of the black church if you were classified or described yourself as black, African-American, Negro, or Afro-Caribbean, or you were a descendent of any of the peoples who were citizens of indigenous to the continent of Africa and emigres to the United States, then you were a member of the black church and all of its iterations. Period.

Then it hit me like gas caused by some authentic hot chicken from Nashville, Tennessee. This black church as described by Dr. Glaude, the nebulous entity, in the general sense is dead. The church I used to attend was dead to me. Were there some corollaries in his article that I could explore and substantiate my own feelings on the demise of the black church? Just so you know, I did attend some other non-traditional, non-denominational "mixed" congregations but found that these supposedly diverse congregations and their structures were totally reminiscent of my experiences in the black church. I doubled down and was still left wanting.

Now before y'all close this book, click on a new website or say something disastrous, let me clear a few things up. I said the black church is dead to me. There, I said it. That's strictly my opinion. I only capitalize the first letters of the words Black Church here for effect and faux obeisance for the readers who still believe the black church is the center of power, omnipotence, and goodness for all people of color. Next, I am not a Satanist but I do believe in the existence of evil.

Just because I am denouncing the existence of the black church does not mean I have literally become a worshipper of evil, merely a seeker of the truth.

Finally, I said that the black church (local, community-based worship) is dead to me. I said the church—the building, the assembly, the notion, and its traditions and practices mostly traditional and mostly contrived in order to maintain fealty and obedience and fear—was dead. I did not perversely state as Nietzsche did that God is dead.

Now before you begin to put me in the same "he goin' to hell" lane as Dr. Glaude, I want you to remember something that touched me and is the impetus for me making my statement: "He whom the Son sets free is free indeed."[2]

As a part of this freedom, the Son grants you discernment and wisdom about your present and future course of action. Although mine came with a lot of baggage, I believe that I was also granted time to evaluate what I believe and why I believe as a man of color and as a minister.

Now, the black church as I define it is the collective assortment of people of color who worship the Judeo-Christian god and have the belief in the complete and utter truth of his Word as encapsulated in the Holy Bible as both anchor and compass for our journey through this life with instructions on how to attain eternity when we die. The black

---

2 John 8:36 (New King James Version).

church in theory emphasizes equality among men, helps ameliorate the conditions of the poor and downtrodden and possesses an unwavering commitment to social justice in the communities the church serves. It was this unifying belief in Jesus Christ and his teaching of long-suffering, faith, and deliverance that emboldened black Americans to demand equal rights. The black church as I define it generally and simplistically is comprised on the whole of black Americans who express a common belief in Jesus Christ and explicitly emphasizes equality and unwavering commitment to social justice for all black Americans, specifically for civil rights.

When I think of the black church, it comprises more than several people of color congregating to a building in a community with a pastor and deacons, choir, auxiliaries, pastor's and deacons' wives, meetings, and all those other similarities found in the order of service, including method of worship, style of music, clothing (oh, the clothes), and style of preaching.

The black church to me is an institution greater than the sum of its parts that tackles first and foremost, issue of salvation and faith then assists the carnal mind, i.e. black Americans in their struggle for equality in the areas of housing, economics, recidivism in incarceration, education and the basic treatment of minorities by the government and their agents. In my mind, Jesus Christ was a radical and had not a "by whatever means necessary" attitude about expressing his father's will but a "this is what it is, and there is no other way but through me" attitude.

The black church in effect takes those collective teachings from the New Testament, showing the civil disobedience of Jesus and his followers engaging in acts punishable by the Roman law at the time. For example, Jesus and his disciples stole crops and at corn[3] on the Sabbath, engaged in the unauthorized healing of paralytic outside the temple gates without priests' approval,[4] allegedly sowed dissension among the people with talk of a Savior[5] and the crime for which he was ultimately killed: sedition.[6]

Additionally, coupled with the stories showing God's love and wrath (more often than not) from the Old Testament as Jesus's mission to free his people and future generations from the shackles of sin to enlightenment by the Great Commission,[7] so the black church stood as the epicenter of the civil rights movement because only commonality of belief and power of God coupled with the multitudes of women and men of color across the United States engaging in acts of civil disobedience and peaceful demonstrations with whites could have

---

3 Lev. 23:3, Deut. 5:12–15, Mark 2:23 (King James Version).

4 Matt. 21:12–16 (King James Version).

5 Luke 23 1–5 (King James Version).

6 Matthew 26:59-66; Resa Aslan, Zealot: *The Life and Times of Jesus of Nazareth*, pgs. 174-175. 2013.

7 Matt. 28: 19–20 (King James Version).

caused a change in this country that led to legislation being signed by then president Lyndon B. Johnson effectively ending segregation.[8]

The black church of the Civil Rights Movement is akin to the Moral Majority, that powerful evangelical turned political construct created by Jerry Falwell in 1979. Their mission statement: "to reverse the politicization of immorality in our society." Their most powerful weapon was influence. Victories attributed to their influence included the election of George H.W. Bush in 1988, several Supreme Court decisions and influencing the creation of the Christian Coalition.[9]Aside from the Civil Rights Movement, what has the black church accomplished as an entity since 1965 on a national level? And don't tell me the election of Barak Hussein Obama as the first African-American president in 2008.

To understand the concept of the black church is to understand church as blacks see it, or as this black man sees it, and how the church has been laid out to me since I accepted Christ at the age of 12 and attended churches well into my adult life comprised of all black or predominantly black congregants until 2008.

Every predominantly black church in America during the civil rights movement became its own ground zero in the fight for equal rights. Its members and attendees were denied equal treatment outside of its four walls.

---

8 Voting Rights Act of 1965.

9 "Moral Majority Founder Jerry Falwell dies" . May 11, 2007. Associated Press. Nbcnews.com

On the inside of the church, although there was a hierarchy of sorts, there was also a common enemy: white America. Jim Crow and segregation and an unjust legal system and a general mien that blacks were inferior intellectually and morally were outright justifications for white America to feel the way they felt, but the hatred and vitriol that accompanied those justifications, especially in locales such as Birmingham, Alabama, and Jackson, Mississippi, were so much that the church was indeed a refuge.

These churches would teach nonviolence, and began the practice of looking out for one's own despite the evil in the hearts of their peers, and educating and marshaling resources so as to one day intelligently combat the myriad and seemingly unopposed and relentless vicissitudes of daily black life.

It was in this commonality of suffering within the black community, even with exceptions in skin color, economic influence, and intraracial divides, that the black church was born and was visible to the nation.

However, post-civil rights, the black church has become something more akin to a minstrel show. You have that group of friends who you haven't seen for a while, and you all can sit and talk about the goings-on in your particular church or place of worship. There are many, many similarities. However, there are some practices that are endemic to that particular congregation—some scriptural, some personal, some traditional, but mostly traditionally bad and invasive.

I have seen a gradual "falling away" from the church, not the falling away as described by most ministers as evil people becoming heretics and denouncing Jesus. The falling away is from churches and their hypocrisy and their outdated traditions and failure to embrace logic and questions about their beliefs.

So let me start at the beginning, so you will get an idea of where the impetus of the book lies so you can follow along. Prepare yourself.

What I am about to disclose to you goes against everything that I formerly held dear, yea, even considered sacred to a black southerner who attended a Baptist church. In preparing to write this book, I was accused of attacking the black church by a minister. Several ministers and laypeople were very concerned about me "writing another book about the black church."

These folks believed that the church was and is above reproach, as if it had some inherent wealth and, like the Catholic Church, had its own real-life second-to-none-but-Jesus holy man, the pope. If you are sensitive to anything "un-Jesus" or "antichurch," thank you for your investment in this book, but you may as well just shut it down now. I am only relaying the facts and just the facts from my experiences about the black church and the church, and I expect there to be backlash and condemnation, but my fingers are doing the walking, and my spirit is doing the talking!

The purpose of this book is to show the twenty-first-century church that as my experiences in the church (which was predominantly black) as a microcosm of the term used by Dr. Glaude, *black church*, are corelated and advance my point that the *black church* is dead.

That's right. I said it. The black church as I know it died a long time ago. There is no rescuing that old venerable institution. The notions of going to church Sunday and for Bible study on Wednesday night and double services on Sunday and all of the auxiliaries—Easter Sunday sunrise service, the Christmas program, Christmas speeches, vacation Bible school, revivals, more meetings, haughty preaching, shouting in church in the spirit, choir songs with an extended and remixed ending, long-winded prayers, soul-stirring devotions, the symbolic opening the doors of the church for those seeking baptism, prayer, and membership, and Sunday school ...

It's dead, and I hope to never see you again!

There is nothing left there to rescue!

That was intense for me. I never thought I would say this in my head and heart, much less write it down for people to see. But that is my truth. The black church is dead, but if you want to attend a service for the sake of nostalgia, then go for it. The song "For the Good Times" as sung by Al Green comes to mind when I think of it. It's the song of two consenting adults who have tried to coexist and make something better of their relationship, but time after time, they merely cannot. They have nothing to hold onto but the memory of being intimate, the memories of earnest seduction and lust for that picturesque moment during coitus when all of their desires for each other manifested into something pure, an ultimate expression of their feelings for each other. The world will keep spinning after all.

However, there should be something constant about religion, especially when it touches a community and is so intrinsic in a community such as the African American community, as a standard for righteousness and purity in a world that doesn't make sense.

In a world where an entire race of people was subjugated for centuries and treated as nonhuman, as commodities, there has to be something that keeps us from losing our ever-loving minds. We cannot change history, but we can learn to live and thrive for the good of all humankind but our common belief system. However, when that system has been abused, misinterpreted, and overinterpreted to the point where you don't know who to follow and everything and everyone is under intense scrutiny, it's time for some type of church, some structure, that collects our commonality of beliefs without further dividing us, and it should exist without explanation or subjugation of its adherents.

However, this structure, which most will by default call a "church," this newly evolved organism can be changed and rescued as long as you are giving the people what they need without them seeing the continuing hypocrisy and in-fighting between tradition and hyper-religiosity.

This new church for the twenty-first century will surely follow the demise of its predecessor if it does not (1) get out of its own way and become more transparent and less judgmental in its dealings with the very same people it claims to have a mission to save (rampant hypocrisy and tradition and cult of personality worship), (2) accept the existence of and create different vehicles to carry out the great commission to all people of all nations, and (3) take the necessary steps to bridge the ever-widening chasm between generations of the church for spiritual advancement (in ways other than music or conforming to them—instant pandering).

I will pause to give you, the reader, a chance to bow out gracefully now.

1

ALLOW ME TO INTRODUCE MYSELF ... TO MYSELF

In the beginning I was raised in the church—a native Arkansan, born and reared, and later acquainted with Jesus Christ in Mississippi County. Cotton was the cash crop at the time, and although we were desegregated, there was still institutional racism, classism, and intraracism where I lived.

Our mother made a point of making all the children attend church. She never made it an ultimatum and never directly expressed why we should attend; we just did because it was beyond our ability to resist. I never understood until much later, despite her protestations, why my father did not attend church with us. It wasn't until much, much later in my life that I understood.

My maternal grandfather, however, God rest his soul, made no bones about why he did not attend church. He believed that it was a money-making enterprise and took too much time away from people's real lives. Now in the South, the church *was* a very real part of people's lives, right down to the many programs, assemblies, ministries, meetings, auxiliaries, afternoon programs, worship programs, friends and family days, visits with other churches (same denomination, mind you—wasn't any mixing!), and, finally, raising money for the "building fund"!

It didn't help that my grandfather was a raging alcoholic and an avid baseball fan. He loved the Atlanta Braves most of all, but I believe that is because he almost always had the channel tuned to TBS Superstation, the Ted Turner-owned station out of Georgia that we viewed most frequently. His vitriol and speeches on Sunday afternoons when we would walk our grandmother from church are the stuff of legend and comedic genius.

My grandfather would often have in his hand a large dark cup of alcohol, and he was also a chain smoker. He sat with his legs crossed and apparently could not wait until we all arrived at his home in order to eat a home-cooked, after-church meal at my grandmother's home before we went to our home to eat another meal of our mother's food.

He would excoriate and mock my grandmother's unflappable obedience to God—and, more importantly, to the pastor and the church. My grandfather remained the same even after I left for college. In his last days, I did not sense any sort of repentance or remorse about his unchronicled experiences with the church or about his oft-anticipated monologues about churches and their insatiable need for your time and your money. To this day, I have no idea where it all came from. But as I said, his tirades were the stuff of legend!

Once we were at church, all the *-isms* I referenced earlier, all the awkwardness, and all my actual or imagined inadequacies disappeared—and I learned to love Jesus.

But before Jesus, I was regaled with the Old Testament prophets and their indoctrination into the causes of doing what God told them to do for His glory, and their willingness to serve.

Samson, David, Elisha, Elijah, and Moses. It helped that I was a great lover of fiction and a burgeoning avid reader—especially comic books. I was reading about the archetypes of some of the greatest superheroes of Marvel and DC comics such as Superman (Samson) and Batman (Moses, and his staff); only the Bible was real.

Because I was such an avid reader, I digested these stories and began to build the foundations of my belief in a higher power—a power greater than myself. The physical church, the building, was where my belief was fomented and expressed without fear, rejection, or ridicule. As such, I became the youngest assistant superintendent in that building's history.

Let me stop for a moment and clear something up. I am purposely distinguishing the word *building* from the word *church* because I believe the church is comprised of the actual human believers of Jesus Christ as expressed in the scriptures[10]; it is not the myriad denominations and buildings that saturate our American landscape.

Let's face it. These buildings are ubiquitous in the black church community: they come with the standard crucifixes affixed atop the building, or they have one of those eight-foot-tall Sam's Club crucifixes on the church grounds. And there's an obligatory sign stating the title of the church, the hours of operation of Sunday school and worship services, and the pastor's name—and in some iterations, the names of the associate ministers (less commonly) and the name of the wife of the pastor (more commonly), who was titled at some point as the "first lady." I don't specifically remember or know the origin of this designation as it relates to black church bodies; nor do I understand its rise to prominence, relevance, or reverence in the black church. But at this time I will state a recurring theme that has no biblical or spiritual rhyme or reason with many things currently found in this exploration of the black church: *it just is!*

I was still the youngest superintendent in the church's history (ten years of age), and I was having a ball. I was quoting the scriptures and regaling my peers and my older contemporaries with my understanding of the principles of God's ultimate authority; I shared the lessons that He provided in his Bible and spoke about how they assisted us in our daily lives.

---

10 1 Cor. 12:12–14, 27 (King James Version).

The fire and brimstone sermons of the pastor added to my own understanding. This black preacher, his son, and others would go into the pulpit—a place we were taught to never ever enter. By this time, I had seen the Easter classic film *The Ten Commandments*, directed by Cecile B. DeMille and starring Charlton Heston as Moses and the great Yul Brynner as Rameses.

A scene that continues to captivate me to this day was when Moses appeared before the burning bush, and the voice of God told him to take his sandals off his feet because he stood on holy ground. Moses's fear and obedience at that moment resonated with me, and for several years after that, every time I walked by the pulpit, I had that fear. Even if someone told me to grab a fan or get a water tray, I stood with fear and trembling because I literally thought I would hear that same voice and face some type of curse by setting foot on the pulpit because of my unholiness.

So there I was, between being accepted by this group of believers and having a place where I was not mocked or was pleasantly mocked, depending on the day, because of my race, size, where I lived, or how I dressed. There at the church I was doing something and believing in something that transcended all of those petty human beliefs. Why not love Jesus the way He showed love for me?

I was baptized at the age of twelve because I just believed there had to be something greater—something better—and my actions and my life at that time were defined by it. I had several talents, and I was going to use them for the greater glory of God by serving in as many capacities as I could in the black church I attended.

My belief system at that time in my life as a big black southerner helped me get through a very rough and confusing childhood. My size and my ethnicity were the only stereotypes that were spot on at that preteen-to-teenage stage in my life. I was an avid reader of comic books, loved music, could sing first tenor, and was deathly afraid of women. I was not a particularly great athlete because I cared more about reading and girls than I did sports. And this was partly because I believed most athletes were not the most educationally adept people at my school.

For the most part, they were braggarts who could not cut it in school but had enough physical prowess in their respective sports of choice that it endeared them to the female populace of my junior high and high schools.

What did I have to offer? I could sing, but I was too shy and awkward to engage in any lengthy conversation about what the females were interested in because they quickly grew bored of me. I was too shy to sing to them publicly because I was just "too big to be singing that high," which was a common phrase I would hear from people. Plus, most of the crew I hung out with were athletes who would rib me from time to time about not playing football very well but singing like a bird. I tell you, some nights, if it had not been for the Lord on my side ...

My belief, attendance at church, and getting around a church crowd were the only things that stopped me from getting too depressed. At church, I was lauded and supported because I could speak and sing freely, and I was only judged on how I treated my peers and the elderly at the church.

There were times, however, that I wanted something more. There were ... incidents ... snippets of gossip ... about the pastor's philandering, about children out of wedlock, about fornication, adultery, and mental illness, and about other things that I chose to ignore because I believed they would have destroyed what I wanted my church to be. All the evils and deception that existed outside of the church had come into the church, making my church no longer a safe place for me anymore. I consciously disregarded these rumors and steered clear of them because I could not have gone another step further. I mentally did the physical equivalent of putting my fingers in my ears and shaking my head from side to side, frantically shouting to keep all outside noise from piercing my ears. I didn't know it then, but this is what the black church had been doing for years.

I had no idea how much it would affect me until much later in my life.

2

GROWING UP GOSPEL

As I grew older and looked back, however, there were a lot of practices that confused me and had no place in my religious experiences. Here are just a few.

I am a native southerner, born and raised in the Mississippi Delta in northeastern Arkansas. We were forced as children to attend church by our mother. There were certain religious practices that we were taught early on that were the surest way to Hell. The first was "do not step in the pulpit." That's right. The pulpit sat on a raised dais of the church between the choir stands. The superintendent desk, you know, the big desk that offering plates and communion plates were set upon under a sheet, sat before it, and in the pulpit, of course, was the pastor/ preacher's lectern.

We were chided even during choir rehearsal to go around this "holy ground," otherwise we would incur the wrath of the Lord as well as our parents or any adults around who witnessed such an affront to church tradition and etiquette. Even if church was not in session, you could not traverse or even play upon the steps leading up to the pulpit.

Another practice I saw in the church was forcing pregnant teens to sit on the front row of the church before the congregation on a particular Sunday and publicly condemn them for having intercourse. Because of the gossip in the church, everyone knew who was pregnant and who was having relations; it was just the nature of things. However, when, apparently spontaneously, you make these young girls go before the church and sit in public view of members and visitors and publicly humiliate them *with* parental consent, it was horrible! I don't quite remember the young men being called to the front of the church in the same fashion, but I was embarrassed for the girls and knew better than to ask for a reason for such practices.

Another holy and traditional practice that has been the subject of contentious and raucous debate in the black church, second only to paying the pastor/preacher, was tithing. In all my years of attending church, I never quite understood why I had to pay a tenth of my monthly gross pay to the church. All I know is that you were in danger of being killed by God or facing financial ruin if you did not tithe.[11] And somehow, the pastor knew if you were not tithing. Then the church would find out about you not tithing. As I got older, I knew of some

---

11 Mal. 3:8–12 (King James Version). "Will a man rob God?"

local area churches that would post delinquent tithers' names in the open as if they were exam scores in the church.

Now this is an example of how deathly egregious nontithers were considered. In 2006, I asked an older churchgoer about the reasoning behind the whole church tithing and my personal intentions to ask the pastor of the church I was attending how the collected tithes were utilized. This person informed me that she actually questioned the pastor about the dispensation of the tithe, and days later fell ill to a mysterious disease that left her in pain. She took it as a sign from God that she did not need to question the pastor, as he was responsible to God alone and did not have to answer to a member about church finances.

I was appalled, and it really took everything I had not to laugh in her face. She was deathly serious about being stricken with a disease. Almost every member I questioned about this issue of tithing and pastoral accountability gave me the same response: "If there is malfeasance, God will put a stop to it. We can't worry about it. Let God handle it. I'm just going to do what the Bible tells me to do and let the pastor be answerable to God."

As I became older, I noticed a control structure within the church that started and ended with the pastor. I would hear of my mother's consternation about having to tithe more than once during service. However, that was quickly cleared up, as every subsequent request for money was quickly categorized and its purpose was specified before those trays came out again.

There were times, in retrospect, where I believe the pastor would make people walk up to place money in the plates in order to embarrass them before their peers for not believing and trusting enough in God to return to them what they were willingly giving to the church.

In 2011, I sent out a survey to various member churches of the National Baptist Convention, and one of the questions concerned tithing. As in real life, the questions about God and money and church in that combination are anathema to church, as poisonous as ultraviolent rays are to vampires, silver to werewolves, water to fire; you get the idea. Any concern about money and where it went after it left your hand and went into the offering plate was deemed nearly heretical in the church I grew up in and attended as a young adult.

As a child, I was waylaid with the story of the god born as a man who loved me so much and endured so much physical suffering as an expression of love for all humanity that he willingly allowed himself to be put to death for the further propagation of humanity as it exists today. *Wow!* Being on the lower end of the financial spectrum in Mississippi County, Arkansas, where racism and classism and intraracism were parts of my everyday life, to go to church and be told of love like that was simply mind-boggling. Give me some of that! Jesus?! I will take it! What do I have to do to join that band? Who do I have to kill to get me some of that?!

Essentially, though, time passes and the world moves on; there have been certain paradigm shifts with the black church as a whole and within individual black churches as its members sought only approval from the pastor as the only source and inspiration for church action as opposed to the will of God. I believe the quote that the Word is the same yesterday, today, and forever." As I became older and matriculated through life from high school to college, I still believed, but I was ill-prepared to deal with the world on its terms.

Instead, I contrived a way to deal with people as I had been instructed to by the Bible. However, a funny thing happened. I found that there were many times I would deal with people, real churchgoing people such as myself, who shared a zeal and a common belief in God, who treated me just as poorly as those who were "of the world." If we all looked at the same tome and shared the same disadvantages and trials and tribulations of this life when we agreed to follow Jesus, should we not recognize each other from the world? Should we not reach out and assist those like-minded individuals first? Should we not have some honor?

I have learned that even though this country was founded on "Christian" principles, although our currency has the slogan, "In God We Trust," there is not equality on this earth when it comes to Christians or believers. It was around this time, after I got married and attended a church for nearly seven years, when I received my *real* education about the business of Christianity and the business of black church so that I no longer took to the appellation of "Christian." I didn't even feel comfortable saying the word "Christian" anymore because to me that was a connotation, a wink that I had assimilated into this business of hat wearing, tithing, slogan-speech, anthem song-making, shouting, Jabberwock speaking, highly traditional, Matrix-frenzied community of black church that was being boxed and shipped to the masses of America and beyond. It was during this time I began to enter the dark night of my soul.

3

THE DARK NIGHT OF MY SOUL

At the beginning of my divorce in 2006, I entered into the private practice of law. Beforehand, I was a public defender, trying to learn my craft, and was a devout member of a predominantly black church in Kansas City. During this time, I never felt closer to God. I had nothing else to fall back on. Somehow, someway, I survived. My personal life survived. My prayer life became a bit more complicated.

I was a deacon, a singer, a teacher, and an associate minister. However, something was lost in translation. Something was lost between what I was reading and how business was being conducted in the church I was attending. I sought answers from the pastor about these issues of faith and application in the business of church, but it was not easy to schedule an appointment with due to constraints on his time. Quite frankly, I knew the pastor and I were not going to see eye to eye on many of my questions but I had to meet with the pastor, nonetheless.

I then sought the confidential counsel of older gentlemen who I attended church with and who I believed were wiser and smarter than me because of their age and experience. My questions were from a troubled heart and spirit. I was trying not to expose anyone or call anyone out, but I needed clarification, and if, from my questioning, one could discern that I was overextending my reach or was completely out of line, I could be corrected by him before the ultimate confrontation at some point with the pastor.

I asked for wisdom and understanding. I literally prayed that the scales would be lifted from my eyes.[12] When I asked for Truth, and sought Truth in what I was doing for God, it hurt. It hurt worse than the divorce. This severing of me from the black church was on top of a divorce. It was a double death. I saw the black church as a business and not as a place for the fallen, the weak, and the heavy-laden. It was no longer a refuge. It was a club. It was a business. It was a hierarchal system where the pastor was the CEO and certain members of the church, the entire finance committee, and the deacon board (of which I was a member) were all the executives. This church that I freely worshipped at, cried to, sang and shared inspired personal stories of faith and perseverance and Jesus, had become a *business*.

I was made privy to some discussions about members, not about spiritual matters, but about real world issues such as benevolence,

---

12 Acts 9:18 (King James Version).

and donations to the poor and charities, and financial decisions with tithes and money that we donated. All the power, all the solemnity, all the holiness and reverence had been stripped away to one person deciding who gets what and why and if you had a problem with it, you had to go through a huddle of other Christians to question the pastor, the undershepherd.

I was having a crisis of conscience because I did not know how I continued to exist in this new world. I could no longer sing or sit in the pulpit because I asked for Truth. Truth was not "The Old Ship of Zion," nor was it to be found "Near the Cross." Not for me. Not any longer. The Truth I sought was how could something so pure, so inspiring, and so powerful, become so corrupted that those who grew up as I did could not see this abomination.

Those who grew up as I did could not see this deformed, mutated *thing*, call it of God, and not immediately call a meeting in the church during Sunday morning service and exclaim that "this is not what Jesus intended!"

Night had fallen in my life, and I was upset that I had asked the Creator to show me the Truth. Better had I remained in ignorant, compliant conformity than to now be on the outside. However, "love said not so," and I was shown my strength and my purpose, and steeled my resolve.

I once read a statement from a book where one character said to another, "your weight is your heart." When asked by the hearer what the speaker meant, the speaker replied, "You feel things maybe more than you should. There are circumstances in which that could make things very difficult for you."[13] This statement describes to the penultimate "tee," the tip-top. This is who I am; this is who I believe I shall always be.

Several months later, I had a private confrontation with the pastor of the church. It began as a letter between us that was several pages long. In that letter, I basically asked the pastor to reconcile the practices he was implementing in the church with the Holy Scripture. I even asked for a private lunch or dinner meeting, for him to explain his response.

I handed the letter directly to him and gave it to him under the proviso that he may be upset, but I needed to get answers from the highest authority in the church that I knew. My hope was that he would understand and either tell me the Truth or tell me that I was out of line. Either way, I could no longer sit back and operate the same way I had been in the previous years. I was a minister, for God's sake. I received my calling from the Creator, and I had to understand what I was doing. Charity starts at home after all, right?

Weeks after the pastor had read my letter, my personal entreaty to him for answers about church practices, policy and procedures, the pastor called me to schedule a meeting with him.

---

13 Terry Hayes, *I Am Pilgrim*, Simon and Schuster, London pg. 367.

He admitted to me that he was quite upset with the content of the letter. I then told him that is why I asked for a lunch or dinner setting to discuss it. He insisted we meet at his office. To my consternation, I told him that "I have an office, too," as a way of letting him know that I was not intimidated if he was angry. Nonetheless, I relented and told him we could meet in his office.

When I arrived with notepad and Bible in hand, he had all seven pages of my letter spread out facing him on his desk with passages underlined and arrows drawn in the margins and highlighted areas of the letter. He *did* read it, I said to myself.

The meeting started out harmlessly enough, but there was a knock on his door, and a senior deacon entered. The pastor told me he wanted a "witness" present and hoped that I did not mind. I wanted to protest, but I had nothing to fear, as I wrote the letter not to assault the pastor but as a person who needed some things clarified. However, the attorney in me sensed the burgeoning pulse of a verbal atomic bomb that was primed to go off at the slightest misgiving.

I will not go into the blow by blow of the meeting but I will reiterate to you that my intentions were noble, and I believed coming to the pastor in this way was better; attempting to foment a rebellion by way of gossip was not the Christlike way to get the answers I desperately desired. Now I can and will tell you the series that lit the fuse, but only on condition of anonymity.

Pastor: Now you know that I have been teaching a class here every third Sunday. You don't attend the class.

Me: You have known for the longest time, or should know, that every third Sunday I go to visit my son out of town. That is my visitation weekend.

Pastor: How is that my problem?

To put this in its proper context, I had already felt that the church, which had a lot of resources, was not doing enough in the community to assist others in the areas of evangelism and community outreach. I had felt that the spirituality had been bled out of the church behind hyperbole and that the congregation was of the belief that if you want something better, then you need to come to our church. The entire demeanor of the church had evolved from one of humility to arrogance. It turned into a King Saul before my eyes in a few years because we had managed to build a huge edifice, the first of its magnitude by a twenty-first-century predominantly black church in this county.

However, the church had lost its very raison d'etre, and it became all about people coming to join the church and enjoy the fancy ministries. The little man became lost in the shuffle. It was lip service at best. Every ministry that I believed should be started or should be handled in a more Christlike manner was now subject to red tape and to the dictates of one person: the pastor. I believed the church had fallen under the auspices of a megalomaniacal dictator, and we lost our way. It was all about the money. I wanted to know the Truth from the lips of the pastor. Had this church become just another song and dance number, to be grouped in with all of the other institutions prostituting Christ and doing it with impunity? Where was the Truth? Was I wrong? Did this church no longer care?

So when the pastor uttered that final question, "How is that my problem?" my path became clear. It wasn't the pastor's problem to fix, per se.

The pastor could not "fix" anything; it was my purpose.

I know. You are probably thinking that this guy has gone from nearly unheard of black atheist devolution mode to the Dan Ackroyd / John Belushi line uttered with all deadpan seriousness from the classic hit *The Blues Brothers*: "We're on a mission from God." If you believe in something, then stand up for what you believe in, and nourish it, support it, and let it flow. Drug dealers believe in making money and have no qualms about who they hurt. Politicians and public figures and celebrities say what they want without fear of reprisal and get their message out there. Who am I not to do that?

4

THE POWER OF PURPOSE

This was no overnight thing.

Initially, I was gung ho, and believed that there had been such a massive abuse of power in the black church community that I was going to be the one to enlighten others and empower them to demand changes within their churches. It all started with accountability. Who was going to be responsible for this change from traditional to progressive thought? Who was responsible for the current state of affairs in the black church? The pastors.

At first, I believed that I had to find a new "church home." I decided to cut ties with my old church, and engaged in the practice negatively described and decried by church folk called "church hopping." For those of you who are unfamiliar with these two terms, I will explain each in turn. In the black lexicon, "church home" basically means the church where you pay your tithes regularly or semiregularly, where you want not only an accounting to God for your monies, but where you can receive your charitable donations form for tax-filing season. It's also where you spend the majority of your Sundays around people and a preacher that you both like and get along with. If you are going to be out of town or plan on visiting another church as a visitor, you must give the pastor notice that you won't be attending your regularly scheduled church service and that he knows when you will be back. Otherwise, the pastor will call your name during service or be on the lookout for you because he/she doesn't want to lose the faithful, tithe-paying members.

The home church is the church where you have generated relationships with people you see on a more pleasant, more similarly situated, more comfortable place than most of the people you work with five days a week.

The home church denotes trust and belief in the pastor's vision of what God has instructed him/her to do as it relates to your church, and his/her "teaching" and "preaching" of the gospel.

It's the church where you and your family have decided to become members and be a part of that specific church community.

Church home is your physical base of operations.

Now church hopping is a term used negatively by the church, notably by the pastor, to describe a restlessness in one's spirit that produces the inability to decide which church home one wants to become a part of.

Many pastors personally do not like church hopping because there is no loyalty where tithing, membership, and overall acceptance to one and only one church (and therefore, Jesus) are present. For the most part, these persons are evading paying tithes or are being indecisive due to their constant struggle against Satan, who is creating this wandering state. It's like the scene from the movie "Bridesmaids" where Terry Crews' character is giving workouts to paying customers in the park and the characters portrayed by Kristen Wiig and Maya Rudolph who have not paid are standing close enough to mimic the exercises the paying members are being instructed to perform. A church hopper basically receives free fellowship, hospitality, sermon and singing from the church but have not made a decision to join and thereafter tithe to that church.

Okay. Now, I decided to attend different worship services, and hopefully during my visits, I would receive a spiritual epiphany and be directed where my ministry would begin. I attended nondenominational churches, Methodist churches, storefront starter churches, and churches that were not predominantly black, but to no avail; I saw the same sycophantic, worship tropes I had been a part of for years.

At every service I attended, I would hear the same catch phrases, this semblance of holiness, this atmosphere of "welcome brother," but there was nothing new under the sun. I was not pushed by this overwhelming desire to join and tell the minister that I wanted to preach or that I wanted to join ... until I went to one other church.

At this church, I was accepted with open arms and allowed to sing and preach without becoming a member of the church. My new mind-set was acceptance of a person despite his membership to *your* church. After meeting with that pastor, I explained my new mind-set—free to worship, loving God and his people—and that should be enough.

That lasted for a few months, and then the pastor and his wife put on a skit in which basically the pastor conveyed to the congregation that he had asked for free maintenance of the church by some of the members who had agreed and then reneged for one reason or another.

The pastor's skit included imaginary members who asked for his services to preach at funerals and see loved ones at the nursing home, and the preacher and his wife basically stating that the pastor did not have time to study and pray for his sermons and provide the spiritual service the others needed because he was busy doing the maintenance duties upon which the people had reneged.

This skit, coupled with the growing murmurings of displeased members asking for my ouster because I had not officially accepted membership with the congregation was the final decisive blow in my attempts to return the church in its present form. There was simply no place for me in organized religion.

I had had absolutely enough of the black church—its traditions, its attitudes, and its nonessential crap. I was focused on the Spirit, right and true, and I was thwarted at every turn.

I was adrift. I prayed, but there was really no belief that things would change. Black churches were too steeped in tradition, the very thing that Jesus warned against.[14]

As I continued in the dark night of my soul and began questioning the existence of God, Dr. Glaude's bold proclamation in 2010 inspired me to begin a quest of my own in determining my religious beliefs. Again, not to change anything, but to merely profess to the world that this entity that we call church has become a business. It is not a house of prayer as Jesus professed when he beat the money changers out of the temple.[15]

Jesus decried that this place was a house of prayer.[16] The Bible was conflicting with the principles that I had unwittingly supported and obeyed for much of my youth and young adult life. The obedience and power the black church placed on me was overwhelming, and not until I had asked for Truth and became disgusted with the assembly line sanctification, clichéd, laissez faire man-structured existence did I know what my purpose was.

The changes that have swept the black community and our county over the past few years have been deplorable. Genocide in Chicago, reality TV, celebrity pastors, the advent of the preachers becoming life coaches, the national debate over the definition of marriage, LGBTQ

---

[14] Matt. 19:1–7 (King James Version) traditions of men over the spiritual of the church.

[15] Matt. 21: 12-13, Luke 19:46 (King James Version)

[16] Matt. 21:12–13 (King James Version)

issues in society, race baiting and criminal justice reform are just a few areas where I have to ask the question: Where is the Black Church?

As a matter of fact, it further encouraged me to do what I believe most people of color at the time were afraid, and in some respects still are afraid, to do: speak out about the growing inefficacy of the black church.

I am not writing a tell-all exposé on all things associated with black religious practices or black thought or anything that in today's reality makes you more or less *black*. I am from a generation and a class of thought that looks at the black church a lot differently than my parents, or my parents' parents' parents. I am of the age where I no longer have to accept certain practical realities of being described as part of the "black church."

Although people of color are as differentiated as their individual experiences, social class, life experiences and spiritual beliefs, I believe from a lifetime of listening and consuming our collective dialogue, comedic aspirations and music that there is a commonality of experience that can be confirmed and attributed to some type of exposure to a predominantly black church.

Now this membership and its "privileges" vary due to size, zeal, and teaching of each church, but when I describe the black church, I mean the institution as it was circa 1628–1990, that bastion of education, community, social justice, and political power that eased hearts and minds and kept our progenitors fixated on a hope that their lives and standing in this country would get better. Better yet, demanded that their status would get better. The birth of the black liberation theology of James Cone,[17] whose underpinning anointed Black Americans as the chosen people of God and that in due time, the sufferings of Black America would be absolved and the Creator would make them magically ascend to their rightful place in the world as well as in Heaven.

However, I no longer subscribe to the victimology inherent in this theology, as it has long outlived its vitality with the ascension of blacks in the public consciousness in the areas of politics, entertainment, and, more acceptably, sports.

Nonetheless, in the latter part of the twentieth century and early twenty-first century, there are still black churches who ascribe to this belief system although they don't acknowledge it as such due to tradition and geography because it has unfortunately become a part of their identity. The church more or less operates in a Matrix-like setting, complete with services, meetings and functions; the church by and large looks foreign to how the Bible describes the church. The problem is that no one seems to want to "pull the plug"—everyone seems content to stay in the Matrix.[18]

I was questioning everything in order to find out who I was in

---

17 Bradley, *Liberating Black Theology.*

18 Mark Lawson, *It's the End of the Church as We Know It* (2007), 40.

this world and whether my centerpiece, the black church, was what I thought it was and continued to be. And echoing the words of the anthropomorphic feline animal: "It's great!"

The black church no longer has a common goal. The black church failed to be relevant because thanks to the men and women in the civil rights movement and upward mobilization of blacks via higher education and exposure, the black church was no longer a single, viable conduit for blacks to get into college and obtain jobs and scholarships and move into the neighborhoods in which they wanted to live.

In order to answer my question about the continued relevance of the "black church," I felt the need to explore the reasons that were provided by this article and explore each one in turn. Dr. Glaude presents three reasons upon which he based his proclamation, each of which I singularly convey to the reader and then posit my three propositions to devolve the church that will rid it of its hypocrisy and confusion to the black, Christian, social-justice-seeking individual and sift through the remains to determine what in the black religious experience is truly worthy to rescue (save) and to recover (nonviable).

5

OLD THINGS ARE PASSED AWAY

DR. GLAUDE'S PROPOSITIONS FOR WHY HE BELIEVES THE BLACK CHURCH IS DEAD

One, Dr. Glaude states that "black churches have always been complicated spaces."[19] Dr. Glaude explains that despite our "traditional stories about them, all too often black churches and those who pastor them have been and continue to be quite conservative. Black televangelists who preach a prosperity gospel aren't new."[20]

Two, Dr. Glaude states that "African-American communities are much more differentiated."[21] The idea of a black church standing at the center of all that takes place in a community has long since passed away. Different areas of black life have become more distinct

---

19 Glaude, "The Black Church."

20 Ibid., 1.

21 Ibid.

and specialized—flourishing outside the bounds and gaze of black churches. Black religious institutions and beliefs stand alongside a number of other vibrant nonreligious institutions and beliefs.[22]

Three, Dr. Glaude claims we have witnessed the "routinization of black witness." Sentences like "the black church has always stood for …" "the black church was our rock," and "without the black church we would have not …" In each instance, a backward glance defines the content of the church's stance in the present."

When I look at all three points, I see a proclamation that basically states that because of rigidity, a conformity to tradition, abuse of power, and relegation of an individual to cult status, the black church can no longer depend on past glories to continue to make it relevant in the twenty-first century. The prospective parishioners of today are in most cases better educated and even more cynical of black churches than ever before, especially in terms of the apparent success of a particular church or minister.

I believe the black church self-destructed on its own as it began assimilation of the doctrine imparted by those before it, especially nonardent believers and, in open desperation, attempted to brainwash a new, more intellectual, yet shrewd generation of followers to drink the same Kool-Aid.

I began to see the conservative manner and actions of the people

---

[22] Ibid.

with whom I formerly worshipped. While at the church during the eight-year period, I became a deacon and also acknowledged my calling to preach the gospel. However, I was greeted with a mass of tradition, things I did not know that went along with the confession of a calling. I felt that more brainwashing was heaped upon more brainwashing.

Wait, that's not true. I believe in a higher power. I believe that Jesus is the way, the truth, and the light. What I was not prepared for was the slowly encompassing rigidity of Baptist tradition when it came to preaching and teaching. Instead of a free-for-all for Christ, there was a line based on tenure and the subjective, *spiritual* discernment of the pastor as to when and where you would preach. I was more than happy to accept the responsibility of preaching and teaching; I was more than happy to begin, but when the "pastoral requirements" of faithfulness, commitment, and attending a Bible college arose, my enthusiasm was diminished because a man was trying to tell me our God told him what to do with me and when to do so.

Again, it got complicated because my heart was not the issue, but the dictates of the pastor won out for no other reason than he was the pastor. My ministry just became more complicated because you minimized it and made it appear to be an audition for the church as opposed to the greater ministry of speaking to God's people from the pulpit.

6

COMPLICATED SPACES

COMPLEX HISTORY OF AFRICANS, AMERICANS, AND RELIGION IN THE UNITED STATES

Look Where He Brought Me From

I would like to address and expound on each of these three points and how they relate to the question posed in the title of my book. Due to the ever-shifting landscape of public life and the advent of social media in the world, black churches are skirting a line to ensure they don't throw the baby out with the bathwater. Complicated spaces indeed.

These complicated spaces within the black church comprise the substance of this book. Of the three points Dr. Glaude pointed to within his essay, the complicated spaces is the one which conjures an image of an anthill that has been stepped upon my someone, and all of the ants therein are scrambling about.

I am in no way calling black churches or those who attend black churches ants, but I am stating that due to the numerous complications that are inherent in Christianity and even in our black churches, I for one have become somewhat confused about what is prevalent and what is merely manna for the masses.

For me, to understand this conservative labeling of black churches as Glaude initially stated in his first point in his discourse is for a person or church to look at the Bible literally in its stories and parables and the very life of Jesus Christ as documented in the King James Version of the Bible.

Now while I am not going to pluck out mine eyes or cut off my hands if they offend me, I did take the opportunity to look from the African diaspora to the antebellum South, the post-Civil War, Jim Crow, and the civil rights movement to determine how we as blacks came across Christianity, and if there were any earlier nuances in black Christian thought as it related to the church.

All of the social mores, the numerous overly holy and sometimes horribly insane rituals observed and taught in just my church that I described earlier in this book are examples of the sophisticated silliness that makes observance and belief in a God of unlimited love and forgiveness so difficult.

Just as the Holy Bible is a complicated book of extremes and often more than not incites further questions about morality and gender roles in society, so does the black church.

As a native southerner, I had been told that historically the black church has been the bastion of our community as it had been set apart and created by a loving and just God to not only tell the Good News of Jesus Christ's birth, death, burial, and resurrection, but to combat social injustices in communities across the American landscape, but first and foremost within the communities in which they are built.

Dr. Glaude comments that this highly conservative view of the Bible as applied within the church has no middle ground and, dare I say, no place in today's American society. With the impetus of Facebook, Twitter, and the advent and dominance of the reality TV shows that leave nothing to the imagination in terms of subject matter, the black church was once held to be the litmus test of the black community.

In much the same way as "black Twitter" serves as a woodshed, grassroots, breathing PSA on all things concerning minorities in the world, the black church used to operate in the very same way.

The strict no-holds-barred, holier-than-thou-precepts of the Holy Bible were used to determine morality in the black community. However, the generation of blacks after the 1960s craved assimilation and integration, and with that craving came a desire to become just like our white counterparts.

Most blacks after the 1960s integration and further into the twenty-first century no longer hold the strict, nonyielding conservative black church standard as their standard. In fact, most have found a newfound spirituality that the black church has not yet learned to embrace or remotely understand.

Many blame the advent of social media, but in reality the black church is steeped in hypocrisy and self-serving attitudes as well as the superstition that if one questions anything by the pastor, that person stands to be cursed physically or financially because of the holiness of the office. These attitudes that I found were prevalent in my southern upbringing from northeast Arkansas are just as prevalent here in the Midwest.

In my opinion, the complications arise when you look to this country's racial past in terms of the institution of slavery. From 1619 to 1968, where was this black church? It existed. Several leaders were steeped in religious fervor, especially when it came to recognizing the humanity of slaves. Most abolitionists saw the humanity in the dusky, bipedal hominid from across the waters, even considering their less than favorable views on the intellectual ability of such a creature. Slaves, Africans, black Americans were deemed human in form but subhuman in their cognitive prowess in comparison to their white counterparts.

In the early seventeenth century, there was no greater travesty in human history than the transatlantic slave trade. The Middle Passage, as it has been known, will forever be known as one of the most horrific yet profitable times of our American history.

An estimated ten million slaves were transported across the

Atlantic Ocean in a period of twenty years, and untold more were lost to sickness, disease, intolerable cruelty, and the viciousness of the crews as they were cast overboard as supplies fell short of demand for both the crew and the living cargo.

While the first slaves arrived in the United States in Jamestown, Massachusetts, more were transplanted down South, where they were quickly driven to become the beasts of burden for which they were originally sought.

Initially, slave masters were reluctant to save the "barbaric, animalistic" Africans for fear they would "take the idea of a messianic figure to liberate them from their hopeless lives of servitude and degradation.

However, slave owners thought it would be a good idea to save these hopeless creatures and give them a reason to stay in servitude to their slave masters, using the Bible as a means of control more than a means of salvation, a trend that continues among black churches today.

Slave owners marveled over the "innate religiosity" of their African slaves as they sought both to tame the savage beast on one hand, and on the other to acknowledge the African slaves' ability to sing, dance, and worship with fervor and vigor, as seen today in churches across America and in just about every gospel song being played on the airwaves today.

It was even proposed in the late nineteenth century that each race brought something different to Christianity when they were converted.[23] Henry Hugh Proctor, as the class valedictorian of the Yale Divinity School, states to his fellow classmates in a commencement speech that Africans brought "humility, fidelity patience, love and large heartedness to Christianity."

As time passed in the South, more social critics, such as Harriet Beecher Stowe, described the relationship between Africans and their quick assimilation to all things Christian as taught to them by their slave owners as romantic racialists.

These racialists did not advocate the freedom of the slave; quite the contrary, slaves were depicted as no more than ignorant savages whom white Europeans brought to the United States to save them from their own savagery by introducing them to their Lord and Savior Jesus Christ.

The term "innate religiosity" was interpreted by Curtis J. Evans to mean two things. One, emotions that were unique to blacks and a complement to the rational faith of whites or the degraded practices of the native slaves that appeared to be what some called religion.[24]

In former president Thomas Jefferson's *Notes on the State of Virginia*, he argued that although black slaves were seriously deficient

---

[23] Curtis J. Evans, *The Burden of Black Religion*, (New York, Oxford University Press, 2008).

[24] Evans, 4.

in "the endowments in the head," they did not lack in the endowments of the heart, particularly in their possession of a moral sense.[25]

It is interesting to note that the same Bible that was used to liberate the souls of the slaves was not used for several decades later to liberate the slaves of the shackles of social segregation and second-class citizenship.

There are many parallels between what the social critics of the eighteenth and nineteenth centuries believed and thought about slaves embracing Christianity and current believers of Christ. As Evans noted, particularly with African American leaders of the time, blacks claimed that the institution of slavery actually contributed to the slaves' moral and spiritual superiority of their white slave masters.

It is ironic to think that such a horrible, devastating series of dehumanization and suffering actually was the work of a Divine Being to instill a place of superiority, albeit spiritual, upon a race of people.

Some black leaders at the time even believed that the sufferings of slavery opened blacks to the workings of divine grace. However, how can all these different races justify the community setbacks that will plague and continue to plague the black community within the United States for centuries to come, even with the knowledge or acknowledgment that blacks were "spiritually superior"?

---

[25] *Thomas Jefferson: Writings*, ed. Merril D. Peterson (New York: Library of America, 1984) as quoted by Evans in *Burden of Black Religion*.

As an average black man living in the United States, more specifically, Kansas City, Kansas, I have become depressed and frustrated on a daily basis as to the plight of black Americans not only in this city but in our sister city, Kansas City, Kansas.

The complication arises from attempts to personally reconcile this country's racial past to the dictates of our churches, our places of worship. While Dr. Glaude merely states that the black churches are "complicated spaces," I don't believe there is a complication at all. I believe that people of color are tired of trying to mentally justify their own personal socioeconomic status with the teachings of Jesus, or as my old school King James Version Bible readers would see as "Jesus' words in red."

The reconciliation is a lifelong curse, a daily tug and flow against self-debasement, and at the end of yet another day's struggle, a denouement of the negativity spewed either consciously or subconsciously by imagery or sound bites of daily existence.

The "waiting on the Lord,"[26] "He will take care of you,"[27] and "he has overcome the world"[28] are juxtapositioned to "when you pray, believe that you have them and you shall receive them."[29] In other words, black folk believe and want to believe, but as we have entered

---

26 Ps. 27:14 (KJV).

27 Phil. 4:19 (KJV).

28 John 16:33 (KJV).

29 Mark 11:24 (KJV).

the twenty-first century, some things are still the same for blacks and have become even worse.

The black church was not ready for the scrutiny of its members and the bigger microscopes that are now centered upon it.

It's kind of hard to justify God when you have been caught with your hand in the cookie jar, and there is no biblical reference to support the pastor or the church.

I have seen churches exist in groups of two to five in a one-mile radius from my home, yet I have no idea what or how these churches are affecting the community at large.

I sometimes found myself echoing the sentiments of Martin Delaney from his book *The Condition, Elevation, Emigration and Destiny of Colored People of the United States* (1852). Mr. Delaney is highly critical of the church, and religion as a whole, as it relates to slaves in that it teaches meekness and servitude to its adherents and to pray to God for deliverance from their involuntary servitude. To not ask questions or smile because it is the "will of God" that you have been subjugated, and only He can deliver you.

In one of his more memorable speeches, Mr. Delaney stated to a group of ministers in Pennsylvania that their sermons to their black parishioners were "stale and miserable doctrines such as the necessity of the colored people for being low, humble, dejected. Low-spirited, sorrowful miserable beings, suffering a life of sorrow in order to get to heaven."[30]

It seems to me that predominant in the religion of Christianity that continues to pervade black church thought today is the laissez-faire dominance of pastors and preachers. No one person in the congregation can ask any questions of the pastor of the church without suffering the wrath of God. A famous phrase used commonly in churches by pastors in self-defense is "touch not my anointed,"[31] a common defense used by preachers in the African American community to prevent any interloper, outsider or member, from questioning any decision or act performed by the minister, as he is only accountable to God.

I often wonder if it occurred to the slaves that the beneficence of the colonizers of the Americas was giving them access to the Great Liberator and at the same time still declaring slavery as permissible and the subjugation of a continent of people as Holy Manifest Destiny.

Religion among the slaves was a mockery of the actions of their masters. However, as more blacks became educated, I believed they wished to reconcile their condition with parts of the Bible they believed were relevant to their plight. Rather than throw the baby out with

---

30 Martin Delaney, *The Condition, Elevation, Emigration, and Destiny of the Colored People of the United States* (1852); reprint, *Negro Social and Political Thought*, 1850–1920*: Representative Texts*, ed. Howard Brotz (New York: Basic Books, 1966), 50.

31 Ps. 105:15 (KJV).

the bathwater, blacks, in my belief, began what I believe to be black liberation theology, which will be discussed in detail later in this book.

Religion, particularly Christianity, was so easy to accept by Africans because it was reasonable to Africans considering their present situation. With sights and sounds and terrifying conditions, debasements of the body, and the outright destruction of familial bonds, the religion as provided by their white slave owners was all that they had to cling to. For their masters, it was the ultimate justification.

It was justification for the system under which they lived. The story of Moses and his leadership under God and his subsequent deliverance of the nation of Israel was analogous to the slaves' plight. Did the slave owners unwittingly give their slaves the keys to their own deliverance?

Was the struggle for equality one that was backed by the slaves' ardent belief in the will of God, or was it one based on morality and human rights? Why did Africans let go of their native religion so easily? I have as many questions as answers.

Proslavery apologists justified the Christianization of slaves by the 1830s on the grounds that it humanized slavery and uplifted Africans from superstition and paganism.[32] Alternatively, their northern counterparts who were antislavery advocates argued that blacks would prosper in a future in which moral sentiment or religious affection was

---

32 Evans, *Burden of Black Religion*, 18.

valued as highly as intellect.[33] So whites generally did not recognize the intellectual capacity of blacks, and indeed agreed generally with the African's inferiority to the majority; however, they believed that the blacks would benefit from religion to save the inferior blacks from themselves and also as a way to "bridge the gap" of inequality between the two races.

Incredulously, both the Old and New Testaments of the Bible contain scripture that advocates[34] and denounces[35] slavery. Now considering the great financial advantages that whites derived from this plentiful and abundant workforce, the obviously smart move would be to teach the slaves that their servitude was *divinely ordained.*

I believe, however, the oppressors were shortsighted in not believing that their slaves would learn to read and also interpret the Bible and find that there were various other scriptures that spoke of "breaking the chains" of servitude of the masters, as once men had claimed a belief in Jesus, all of these men became equal in God's eyes. However, with no short-term way to fight and take their freedom en masse, it took time, patience, and organization.

It is troubling to me that the same divinely inspired book used to

---

33 Ibid.

34 Lev. 25:44–46 (English Standard Version); Colossians 4:1 (ESV); Ephesians 6:5; Exodus 21:20–21.

35 Galatians 5:1 (ESV).

explain and justify slavery could also be used to galvanize a people into action.

The slaves assimilated the church services of their oppressors, complete with their own ministers and choirs. I believe this was the basis for black church as a means to emulate and express what some black leaders of the time believed was a blessing from God: slavery. Southern slavery "relived blacks from a far more cruel slavery in Africa, or from idolatry and cannibalism, and every brutal vice and crime that can disgrace humanity."

The writer further stated that "slavery Christianizes, protects, supports and civilizes blacks. Slavery imposed external control over a people who lacked self-control and who were supposedly dominated by impulse, passion and physical appetites."[36]

Believe it or not, some black leaders of that antebellum South believed that a great gift was bestowed upon blacks via slavery as it opened blacks up to the workings of divine grace. In my opinion, these very thoughts and ideas were the underpinnings of black liberation theology, which is where my biblical indoctrination was initially rooted, and sadly is a strong part of where I believe many black churches, not necessarily in just the South, but all across America, remain to this day.

---

[36] Evans, *Burden of Black Religion*, 47, quoting George Fitzhugh from his book, *Sociology for the South or the Failure of Free Society* (1854: reprint, Wsh. ed. *Antelbellum Writings of George Fitzhugh*) 89, 95.

Enter Black Liberation Theology

This victimist mind-set, I believe, has driven the younger generation away from the black church. Even before the term was coined, black liberation theology was based upon the premise that black folks were the descendants of Moses, and their suffering in the New Word was indicative of their status as the chosen but smitten people of God.

Most people did not know or had not even heard of black liberation theology until President Barack Obama's former pastor, Jeremiah Wright of the Trinity United Church of Christ in Chicago, while in his support of the president in 2008, spoke about blacks suffering in America at the hands of "rich white people."[37] These comments were viewed as racist in speaking out against white America for the purposes of white empowerment.

The term "black theology" is a theology of black liberation. It is the affirmation of black humanity that emancipates black people from white racism, thus providing for both white and black people. It affirms the humanity of white people in that it says no to the encroachment of white oppression.[38]

This term was coined during the civil rights movement when the black church began to focus its attention beyond helping black folks

---

[37] Bradley, Anthony B. Bradley, *Liberating Black Theology: The Bible and the Black Experience in America* (Crossway Books, 2010), 13.

[38] Ibid.

cope with national racial discrimination and move on to applying theology to address the unique issues facing blacks, particularly in urban areas.[39]

Black Liberation theology was a term formally coined in 1970s by James Cone. Dr. Cone developed a doctrine of God. The tenets of his theology were that the Christian understanding of God arises from the liberation of Israel, a God who is actively participating in the oppressed so he could liberate those who are victims of oppression, and God's continual work to assist those who are still oppressed.[40]

The black community, as stated by Cone, "is an oppressed community primarily because of its blackness; hence, the Christological importance of Jesus must be found in his blackness. If he is not black as we are, then the resurrection has little significance for our times."[41] It is Christ's shared victimology that uniquely binds him to blacks, who have suffered under centuries of oppression by whites.

To put a finer point on it, Christ entered the world "where the poor, the despised, and the black are, disclosing that he is with them enduring their humiliation and pain and transforming oppressed slaves into liberated servants.[42]

---

[39] Bradley, at 16 by the National Committee of Black Church Men, 1969.

[40] Bradley, quoting James H. Cone, *A Black Theology of Liberation* (1970) and *God of the Oppressed* (1975), 52.

[41] Ibid, 53.

[42] Ibid., 74, quoting Cone, *Black Theology of Liberation*, 120.

Of course it is understood that God is black as a sign that he has selectively, and thereby actively, wants to free those like him from injustice. In America, the Holy Spirit aids blacks in making decision about their togetherness, which means making preparation for an encounter with whites.[43]

In this sense, a black liberation theory pastor has assured his status as a liberator, as, more likely than not, the pastor will preach a message of commitment from his members to make high financial and spiritual attainment a goal.

Religion had become a nonstop, completely predictable, civil rights movement where the result was never in question. The empowerment of a race of people, righteous empowerment at the humility of another (i.e., blacks over whites), was a national religious movement. You see, the black church became a refuge for slaves as a rejuvenation of their minds and spirits as well as their physical bodies. These slaves were for the most part uneducated and had to rely on the teachings as they were passed down from their masters.

I will say I see it as the continued shoring up of the continued subjugation of slaves, accepting that due to limited resources and development and lack of a strong, nationwide organization, the slaves learned to accept their place and status in American civilization.

Either accept it or risk torture or certain death. This particular black

---

[43] Ibid., 73, quoting Cone at Ibid., 75.

church existed from the mid to late nineteenth century, even after the passage of the Emancipation Proclamation. The black church in the South was just a meeting place where slaves could be slaves, where the men and women and children could learn to govern themselves and craft a hierarchal system within their own community.

These churches for the most part were apolitical; however, that did not stop other blacks from stating their views about the state of black churches prior to the American Civil War. In slavery America, the black church that existed at the time was created to render the Africans docile and resigned to their fate of being categorized as nothing more than chattel, and on the off chance they did have something resembling a soul, a means to accept their role as servants as biblically ordained.

This mind-set changed geographically. In the South, the majority of the ardent but undereducated slaves who were believers clung to the words of the gospel as the law of the land. Therefore, they were content on being the best slaves they could be.

Educated blacks were more often than not critical of the black church as not doing more in their respective communities to make the blacks there speak out more on the conditions and treatment of those under the yoke of slavery, but instead yielding to the scriptures and examples of Jesus Christ's patience and long-suffering at the hands of his enemies.

The conservative, apolitical practices of the black churches were denounced by many black leaders. Booker T. Washington himself did not have a problem with black churches per se but made a profound criticism of black religion, which I believe is relevant to the black churches of today.

In a speech before the National Unitarian Association, Washington stated that the "emotional side of the religion caused them to live in the next world" and that "blacks were fond of singing religious songs and crying out, 'give me Jesus.'"[44] Even in the early 2000s, there were churches that had the "don't worry; Jesus will fix it" mentality. Instead of real answers, the general panacea was "pray and give it to Jesus."

The hypocrisy in the black church again is that if you do as Jesus did (i.e., don't fight your enemies, pray for wisdom and strength, continue to do good, keep the golden rule and serve your pastor and your church), no matter what you are enduring, God will make everything better or will give you the strength to endure.

However, the Bible also teaches that "faith without works is dead" so you better make sure you pay your tithes, and watch and see if God won't pour you out a blessing from heaven! There is some great scripture in the Bible, truly inspiring stuff; however, when your conservative pastor says one thing and does quite another, it can leave you very confused.

---

[44] "A Speech before the National Unitarian Association," September 26, 1894, *Washington Papers*, 477.

The education of the laity, the socioeconomics of the region, the history of the church, the age of its members, its location even, all of these factors alone are significant when assessing the complicated spaces we inhabit.

These thoughts pervade your every waking moment even *before* you join a local church. Once you throw in a little religion and an infrastructure based on allegedly biblical principles, and surround yourself with people who are just as confused or focused on narrow, complex issues of being such as yourself, the disparity in each black community across the nation will change.

Your ability to isolate your feelings and the dictates of your pastor as allegedly inspired and driven by God becomes muddled, and you spend a lot of time trying to please yourself and the church. "Man cannot have two masters."[45] However, the person who wants to please God invariably denies himself or herself and literally take the dictates of the pastor as the word and will of God.

Therefore, the demise of the black church as a group and as an individual entity can be blamed on both the laity who choose to remain sheep to the dictates of a book that they really don't understand because they don't trust themselves, and a pastor who has manipulated the Bible for his own desires and purposes because his ego shall not be

---

[45] Matt. 6:24 (KJV).

supplanted by an individual who surely has no better understanding of the word of God than he does.

THE BLACK THEOLOGY OF TRADITION

Perhaps, the biggest factor in creating these complicated spaces with African American churches is tradition. I have expanded the word *tradition* in this section to encompass intrafaith myths, church codes of conduct, and "Christian" governance. Traditions are for the most part educational to the new converts, as they are supposed to see a progression of the religion in the form of progress for all. However, traditions vary from church to church, and oft times, traditions stagnate and divide a church more than they serve to show a progression to a stronger, more powerful force for change and progress.

For those who will surely be considered rebels or incapable of following the doctrines of their individual churches, the following scripture should be enough to push those against you into the corner from whence they arose. Remember, any believer then can arm himself or herself with these passages to rebuff any advances toward him or her in the name of correction:

1. Then the scribes and Pharisees who were from Jerusalem came to Jesus, saying,

2. "Why do your disciples transgress the tradition of the elders? For they do not wash their hands when they eat bread."
3. He answered and said to them, "Why do you also transgress the commandment of God because of your tradition?
4. "For God commanded, saying, 'Honor your father and your mother' and 'He who curses father or mother, let him be put to death.'
5. "But you say, 'Whoever says to his father or mother, "Whatever profit you might have received from me is a gift to God,"
6. "then he need not honor his father or mother. Thus you have made the commandment of God of no effect by your tradition.
7. "Hypocrites! Well did Isaiah prophesy about you saying:
8. 'These people draw near to Me with their mouth, and honor me with their lips but their heart is far from Me.
9. 'And in vain they worship Me, teaching as doctrines the commandments of men.'"[46]

Traditionally, in the black church, there were not women pastors or preachers. The world of ministry was solely a male-dominated endeavor. The gender of the attendees just so happens to be women, but the leadership positions are predominantly men. I believe the black Baptists are opposed to women pastors because of the admonition of the preacher Paul in his writings about not taking instruction from

---

[46] Matt. 15: 1–9 (KJV).

a woman.[47] Even though this can be challenged in many places in the Bible, as my earlier scripture stated, tradition has held the black church back in most instances.

Women are lauded and congratulated as great single parents but are forbidden by a preacher like Paul to teach a man? Insane. I have never attended a church under the leadership of a female as pastor or had a female preacher. Those progressive minded of us who believe that women should be considered equally in all things are floored by the misogyny of the scripture and the practiced tradition of Baptist churches to acknowledge the intelligence of women.

Some black churches, however, are allowing women to preach the gospel openly and have even taken to allowing the women to call themselves evangelists or prophetesses. A few have gained prominence, such as Shirley Cesar, Yolanda Adams, Kim Burrell, and Juanita Bynum, but in relation to their male counterparts, they are still few in number.

Another traditional mind-set was the advent of women pastors/preachers/teachers in the church. The Bible was very misogynistic. As far as I can remember, the preachers of every church I attended were all helmed by men. The only women of some repute were the wives of the pastors, called the "first ladies."

The book of Timothy, which describes the position of pastor and

---

[47] 1 Tim. 2:11–12 (KJV).

deacon in the traditional church, clearly identifies that either position can only be held by men.[48]

However, when Paul is describing the gifts of the spirit bestowed by heavenly powers, there was no prohibition or proscription against women receiving these gifts or powers.[49] So apparently there is a division in the Bible as to whether a woman can be a pastor or a deacon, but she can receive a gift of teaching and preaching, so therefore she can be a spiritual leader of a church.

Next, the nondisclosure of finances. For as long as I can remember, tithing has been a sore spot in the black church. Although the Bible gives examples of Abraham giving a tenth of what he had to God[50] while he was following God's commandment to leave his home to build a nation, the most quoted scripture has been regarding Malachi and a man robbing God,[51] to promote guilt among the believers. Those members whose hearts were wary of the pastor were given both barrels and were threatened with death if they did not give God his reputedly earned tithes.[52] Threats under this scripture have been levied

---

48 1 Tim. 3:1–7 (KJV).

49 1 Cor. 12:4–10; Eph. 4:11–13 (KJV).

50 Gen. 14:8–20 (NKJV).

51 Mal. 3:6–11 (NKJV).

52 Acts 5:1–11 (NKJV).

against the laity and any nonconforming member of a congregation for not complying with this particular requirement.

The black churches had promoted a feeling of "God justice" if they did not receive the money they believe God was due. Presently, the masses know and understand that their tithes are used to fund the church and pay for its upkeep and for the utilities that they enjoy every Sunday. However, the laity is quiet when it comes to the salaries of the pastor, which their tithes also are used to supplement. The problem with this is that it amounts to slavery all over again.

The complication among black churches is that most of its pastors are full time, and while they do preach on Sunday and Wednesday night Bible study, no one can reasonably justify the salaries and lifestyle many of them are afforded when the members themselves are struggling financially to make ends meet.

Again, tradition coupled with fear dictates that members should blindly give their tithes and, furthermore, not question its usage by the church. Most members don't even have an option to determine to what use their tithes should be put to but are conveniently provided with a tax deduction every year, which they believe counts as their return of their obedience to the scriptures.

Another tradition that has killed the black church is the blind loyalty to its pastors and clergy. The scriptural basis for such loyalty comes from the book of Hebrews.[53] Blind, unthinking loyalty. I have seen it all of my life. Pastors who have whored, stolen money from the church, and acted in ways in public unbecoming to their station have been forgiven and never removed from office in their church. More coups have failed than have been sustained, and more often than not, the at-fault one, even when he has left and started another church, has no shortage of followers.

The dictates of the Bible about forgiveness have been extended to allowing the guilty one to once again preach and teach the gospel to you, and his foibles magnified by the forgiveness of God and illustrated by his feigned admitting to wrongdoing and continued success. However, all other members of the church face losing their position or having their duties minimized for the sake of the church's standing.

Yet another tradition/falsehood is the rights and privileges of membership.

Now I have to take the time here to ask the question: Do any of you who are reading this book have any idea what the rights and privileges of the church (of which you may be a member) are? To those of you who don't understand what I am asking, in the last church where I was a member, there was a point during church service when after the preaching and the hail Mary ablutions of the sinners and saints

---

53 Heb. 13:17 (NKJV).

were in full sway, cue the music, and the minister would ask a couple of questions.

The first question to the congregants would be if anyone wanted to accept Christ as his or her Lord and Savior, then that person should come down to the front of the church beneath the altar or under the speaker's lectern and become a candidate for baptism.

Next, if anyone wanted to come down to the front to join the church based on how he or she was treated on arrival at the church, and the preacher touched him or her in some type of way, then that person would want to continue to become a member of this church and get his or her holy "fix."

Also, there would be a final general category for anyone who wanted to come down and receive special prayer; your reasoning for prayer did not have to be disclosed unless you chose to do so.

Now, if you came down to join the church, you had to already have been baptized. You cannot join the local Baptist church unless you have been "born again." If you have been baptized, no problem. However, if you had not been baptized, you had to confess before a deacon or deaconess your belief in Jesus Christ, and once this was conveyed to the pastor, and the pastor was convinced of your sincerity, then you would be applauded for your decision before the laity and given a schedule for when you would come to church to be baptized.

Now once that hurdle was crossed, you had to discern why you wanted to join this particular church. There were three categories in my previous church: by baptism, by letter of recommendation from your previous pastor, or by Christian experience. Now whichever one of these you chose, the church that you were seeking membership in had you go through a series of classes taught during the Sunday school hours called "new membership" classes. I honestly don't remember what lessons I was taught in my class because it was so long ago. I don't recall if it was a combination of that church's particular history of leadership and activity in that community, and scriptural references to duty and loyalty. I just don't remember.

Now, when you finished this indoctrination, you were paraded down in front of the church at some appointed time to receive the "right hand of fellowship" from the pastor, ministers, associates, and deacons, conferring all rights and privileges of the church.

I have no idea what the rights and privileges were at the church, and to this day, I have no idea, but the black church of the future had better come up with something pragmatic and productive.

Is there a secret handshake, along with some dividends that you are entitled to, and some proprietary interest that you are entitled to for being a member?

I believe the "rights and privileges" are a hoax. You have no rights and privileges. You are paying your offerings to pay property taxes, utilities, and salaries. I say salaries, plural, because most churches don't just have pastors who are entitled to some type of compensation, according to the Bible,[54] but also have secretaries, business managers, janitorial staff, security (for both the pastor and the cars in the parking lot), and in some instances outside specialists who do work for the benefit of the church, such as attorneys and accountants.

So your lauded privilege is one in which you get to mentally take on the duress and burden of paying for domicile and services that really don't benefit you exclusively but the club to which you now belong. If you visit some church in another state or community, do these rights and privileges entitle you to some type of per diem or shelter or some gratuity when you announce that you are a member of another congregation, and just a visitor? Does that mean that this church does not have to turn you away for fear you are an infidel or a nonbeliever?

Not at all. The church can't take a chance on turning away a potential tithing member or another person who wants to suckle the teat of the church to find a sense of community and belonging. So what do these rights and privileges you receive upon joining a church entail?

Absolutely nothing! They are a fiction!

The rights and privileges of the church are, again, just a mind-set

---

[54] 1 Cor. 9:14 (NIV): "In the same way, The Lord has commanded that those who preach the gospel should receive their living from the gospel." Luke 10:7: "Stay in that house, eating and drinking whatever they give you, for the laborer is worth of his wages."

that "hey, you have agreed that in order to come in here and continue to have friends and camaraderie and use the facility during Sunday and Wednesday hours that your financial contributions are paying to maintain, you agreed to be bound under an implied contract because God says it's a good thing to do this."

The last on my list of traditions/codes of conduct is an issue that is not easily answered by the Bible or the black church. It concerns the issue of homosexuality and the way the church has chosen to deal with it on a small and a large scale. In May 2012, President Barack Obama himself admitted he had evolved in his thinking regarding the definition of marriage as being between a man and a woman, and unwaveringly supported same-sex marriages.

Most recently, this part of Dr. Glaude's argument is prevalent in the equal rights movement for the LGBTQ community. As society was bombarded with issues regarding the biblical definition of marriage, those Christian conservatives unashamedly used the same Bible to argue the abomination of homosexuality.[55]

When the issue finally went to the Supreme Court in 2012, same-sex marriage was legitimized by a slight 5–4 majority of justices.[56] Same-sex marriages and survivors' benefits being opened to bullying

---

[55] Rom. 1:26–28; Jude 1:5–8; 1Tim. 1:8–11; Mark 10:6–9; Lev. 18:22; Lev. 20:13 (KJV).

[56] *Obergefell et al v. Hodges*, Director, Ohio Department of Health, et. al. 576 U.S. ____ (2015), 135 S. Ct 2584.

on social media, and the rise of transgender individuals, and questions about gender identity, there arose a massive coming out for various individuals, specifically among those of the faith, believers in Jesus Christ.

For example, societal norms regarding homosexuality within the black community, yea, even the black church, have been crossed, and the church has to decide whether to remain conservative or progressive in its acceptance of the LGBTQ community within the black church.

Now for as long as I can remember, every black church that I was a member of had the following creed: "Love what God loves, and hate what God hates."[57]

The churches to which I belonged operated on a literal interpretation of the Bible as interpreted solely by and through its pastor.

As a native southerner, there was no room for individual interpretation of scripture if you were not the pastor of the church. If the pastor said it, you accepted it and moved on unquestioningly.

Amazingly, as a member of the black church, the pastor's word was *always* openly backed up by the associate ministers of the church; his interpretation was never questioned. (Yep, I did highlight the word "his," as only men were allowed to be pastors in the black church in my early life, a position that is still firmly held today, but I shall address that later.)

---

57 Ps. 97:10 (KJV).

It never occurred to me that the music directors in many black churches that I attended were homosexual. They were magnanimous, eccentric, but outrageously talented people who loved choral music and directing choral music. Many were effeminate, but there was never any open, forward questioning about their sexuality, as it is, or was, a question of privacy.

Their clothing and hairstyles were different and varied; however, they were mostly male and always dressed immaculately. Some even acted effeminately in the way they spoke, walked, and directed, but I never once believed or thought these men who worshipped and "caught the Spirit" and were faithful to the enterprise that is the church choir were people who God allegedly hated and cast out.

When I read the tale of Sodom and Gomorrah in the Bible, all I knew was that God wanted to destroy the city because it was "exceedingly wicked" and its people engaged in all manner of evil. The only reference to homosexuality within that place was when the men of the city surrounded the house of Lot in order to "know" the men who were visitors in Lot's house that evening.[58]

That was my first encounter with homosexuality in the Bible as a youth, and when God sought to destroy that city, I surmised it was based in part on the actions of these men who wanted to gang rape another man. The modern stance of many black churches in the area

---

[58] Gen. 19:4–7 (KJV).

of homosexuality, I believe, comes mainly from the book of Leviticus in the Bible, which states, "Thou shall not lie with mankind as with womankind; it is an abomination."[59] Additionally, it is stated in the book of Leviticus that "If a man also lie with mankind, as he lieth with a woman, both of them have committed an abomination: they shall surely be put to death; their blood shall be upon them."[60]

Dr. Glaude posits that these complicated spaces meant that the black church held fast to its traditional conventions that all things based on, or which became, tradition in the church were the totality of how things were to be adhered. To break it down further, since the traditions of the church were based on the Bible and administered in "decency and order," they were by osmosis the Word of God and the administration of God through the called pastors or undershepherds.[61]

As a young Christian (a designation I no longer choose to be addressed as or ascribe to because of the limitation and denotations that are characteristic within the community in which I live), I have become convinced that the single most common reason blacks belong to churches is to fill some inner longing to be affiliated with "like-minded" people.

Sometimes individuality is a good thing. The Bible states that

---

59 Lev. 18:22 (KJV).

60 Lev. 20:13 (KJV).

61 Glaude, "The Black Church," 2.

we were "set apart"[62] as holy for a purpose, that we are a "peculiar people"[63] and we are not to be conformed to the world.[64]

As to how the black church deals with homosexuality, the Bible teaches only hate and death to those who practice homosexuality. Homosexuals comment that it is not a "choice" or a matter of "free will" to be homosexual; they were created that way. It is in their DNA.

So the black church as a matter of inclusion, I hope in advancing Jesus's example of unconditional love, has chosen not to ostracize homosexuals and allow them to attend church and even hold some positions within the church. Some churches even allow for homosexual marriage, and pastors have emulated their commander in chief in modifying their thoughts on what love as well as marriage should consist of. Should the black church openly query its members about their sexuality and then ostracize them? Should the black church remove homosexuals from their active duties and leadership of certain ministries within their churches?

Should the church fall in line with its president and expand the biblical acceptance of such a lifestyle under the auspices of teaching tolerance and the unqualified love of Jesus? Most conservatives want to adhere to what the Bible says about homosexuality; that is clear. The question remains in the black church, as well as the greater

---

62 Heb. 10:10–12 (KJV).

63 1 Pet. 2:9 (KJV).

64 Rom. 12:2 (KJV).

society: What to do with a homosexual who unrepentantly loves God and wants to serve in some capacity in your congregation and wants to be treated as fairly as you, a minority, does?

Yet another tradition of the church concerns money, but this portion is really trying to ascertain who is getting paid.

Perhaps the most abused persons in the church besides the unknowing and oftentimes lost laity are the ushers and choir members.

The ushers are the lead fodder for the uninitiated and the yellow-shirted security for the pastor who directs traffic. Is either of these positions salaried or hourly? No? And why do neither the ushers nor the choir members derive any money from their service?

As a former choir member, I will tell you why: because we have convinced ourselves that our service is an expression of our love to God and this fabled fanciful obedience to the pastor of the church. We have been brainwashed to serve in the church for free. But what of the pastors, who receive a salary from the church? I am an attorney, and God knows I hear about attorneys' fees and their critiques of overcompensation ad nauseam, but who decides who gets paid in the church?

I know that it is unheard of, but where does it state in the Bible that these are offices where the individual should not or could not be compensated? As a former choir member, and a perfectionist, I know how many hours at church and at home I spend rehearsing the lines to certain songs. The musicians themselves, the instrumentalists, get some type of monetary compensation and in most cases are mercenaries, playing at different churches on a Sunday, earning at least $150 for two to three hours of playing per Sunday.

Again, this figure varies depending on the musician's personal creed about playing for love of God or playing in order to supplement his income and balancing the costs of wardrobe, serving his instruments, and gas.

Would it be so bad if a church pays its pastor, church secretary, minister of music, musicians, and cleaning crew to also pay the choir members or the ushers or even the deacons? Outside of the pastors, who believe themselves to be priests, thereby worthy of their compensation,[65] there are no other scripturally directed officers who are to receive compensation for their work and their commitment to the church.

The first rejection of this ideal would be that it's ludicrous, and it would bankrupt the church. However, if the church is responsible for not only telling the good news but believing it, then the scripture in Luke[66] that talks about giving is appropriate to justify these additional expenditures.

These are but a few of the traditions of black churches that have led to their decline and death. Nonsensical and nonpragmatic ways

---

65 1 Cor. 9:3–10; 12–14; 1 Tim. 5:18 (NKJV).

66 Luke 6:38 (KJV).

of interpreting the scripture have led to a stagnation of belief, a consignment of each individual church to merely seek out like-minded people whose purportedly God-given assignments have relegated them to a cycle of worship, praise, serve, tithe, and repeat. And their own fear and lack of understanding kept them on that wheel.

7

DIFFERENTIATION IN AFRICAN AMERICAN CULTURE

What Works for Me

Dr. Glaude's next reason for his bold statement of the death of the black church is that "African-American communities are more differentiated"[67] The progressive economic and social climb of African Americans in the past fifty years since the end of the civil rights movement has been staggering. In 2008, we welcomed the first biracial president of African descent into office in the United States; the middle class of America has swollen in its growing pains to include a growing number of African Americans who are much more educated and desirous of making a new life for themselves by embracing the

---

67 Glade, "The Black Church," 1.

American dreams of home ownership, and moving from the inner city to the suburbs for better schools and lives for their families.

Accessible education, desegregation, integration, assimilation, upward mobility, and the social connectivity engine called the Internet have enabled blacks to seek a more fulfilling life outside the bounds of the black church. It has brought to fruition the notion of not only having life, but having life more abundantly.

Pastors have seen their dominance and control of your life on Sundays not only challenged by the god of three initials "N-F-L" but a host of nontraditional outlets that allow physical attendance and membership to be minimized and ease the conscience of those who were raised to attend church (a building) with frequency and devout sincerity.

These new and innovative ways brought a change to many African American lives and instilled within these people the desire for a life that, although punishable or frowned upon by the Bible, is a full life engrossed in more spiritually fulfilling matters on a daily level than the usual, traditional, pious black church.

As Dr. Glaude notes, a number of African Americans have flocked to the nondenominational churches helmed by Joel Osteen, Rick Warren, and Jentezen Franklin that often "sound" a lot like black churches.[68] On a personal note, the church I attended became too pious and behaved

---

[68] Glaude, "The Black Church," 1–2.

like a group mind. It was driven by the dictates of one man, who people actually believed was Jesus (or a reasonable facsimile thereof), by the meticulous way he dressed and drove around in a clean car year-round despite inclement weather of *any* kind. The pastor had people carrying his Bible and making sure his robes were laundered and starched in time for service on Sunday morning. It was either an ingenious plan he concocted, or the laity were just a little too naïve. As a former member, I believe it was a little of both.

Don't get me wrong. This is not a backhanded personal attack, but the reality is that a lot of black churches, prominent black churches, are comprised mostly of educated professionals or self-employed businessmen who have made a name for themselves via their education or the influence in their respective positions in their communities (i.e., the black folk who are middle class or upper middle class.

Other individuals who joined these churches were probably not as educated or as materially wealthy as their peers but had a zeal for God and wanted to serve and show service in the church in order to move up the social ladder.

Another segment of this church were those who had long-standing familial ties to the church, such as relatives who were pastors, deacons, or some other high-ranking position in the church, which gave them some type of meritorious membership somewhere above even the richer members of the church and even the pastor. These folks served in positions of influence within the church that kept them in closer proximity to the pastor as opposed to others. Also, depending on the nature of the progenitors' service, these same folks would be president of a particular ministry such as the finance committee, or deacons or deaconesses.

I reiterate, though, that either this was a great business plan or the naïveté of the members. I repeat for myself, though, that it was a little bit of both.

Among the changes this particular pastor implemented were that the duties such as visiting the majority of sick, and smaller emergencies, had been delegated to the deacons. The pastor had to be left alone unless the emergency was of such an extreme nature that he could be summoned from home to pray and lend his spiritual energies to those who were in the hospital or suffered catastrophic injury. Anything else was deemed a job for the deacons or could be put off for another day.

A shift started in the '90s with the nontraditional and traditional black church. The traditional black churches always started with the deacons performing old hymns that were not sung the way the music was written in the hymnals the church provided. This was called the "devotion."

You had a clash of youth versus "experience." Even the implementation of certain choirs began to change in order to appeal to varying age groups. As the music changed and sounded more contemporary for younger crowds, the pastor had to ensure that he appealed to everyone. The black churches had to become one-stop shopping for all of your praise needs.

Early on, the black experience, to be truly authentic, made the church itself a key ingredient. This institution, followed closely by the black barbershop and beauty shop and the dining room table, were the speakeasies of black culture. The wails of the black preacher timed with the organ player created a holy opera. The scale was only limited by the fervor of the audience, which egged the preacher to do more and more outlandish gyrations and vocal inflections to bring home the point of his chosen text for that particular Sunday.

The church became the default entity whereby it was decreed you could only succeed by being a member of it, or as a consequence of your nonconformity, you would not find success.

As I began to study the Bible, I was put off slowly by the dedication of the laity to the pastor, which I saw as a one-way street. It felt as if I had joined a cult. Now, I don't mean to be critical, but I have to be truthful. I was a member of a fairly large Baptist church for almost a decade. Through the years, I felt a slow decline in the individuality of people to come to worship, and I believed the Bible and, more importantly, that the story of Jesus Christ was the story of a liberator, a god who came to the poor, and healed and taught the poor in spirit, and anyone who came had a duty to bless others with his teachings and actions.

It was a freedom of worship and living I had never known before.

I never questioned why I was Baptist or why I had to dress up to go to church or sing the way black churches wanted me to sing or pray the way black churches wanted me to pray. I am a native southerner, and, believe me, I may be biased with this next statement, but southerners know how to have church.

Fashion, entertainment, and a sort of "holy discipline" accompanied every church I ever attended. However, as I became older and began studying the Bible and looking at the story of Christ, it became obvious to me that I was no longer a conservative Christian, and, despite its glowing, shouting appeals otherwise, neither was the black church.

The digression in African American lives varies even more depending on the region, age, education, and traditions of your upbringing, those things that make each individual truly unique. All black churches were not created equal and are not centered on the same goals.

The more exposure you have to the world, the more you end up questioning the things that comprise *your* world. No one could tell me that the black church was the center of the universe anymore. The very scriptures that were being preached to me every Sunday were also the keys to my deliverance. I decided I did not want two masters. I decided I did not want anyone to tell me what was best for me, since God could speak to me as well.

By no means am I implying that all African Americans due to their genetics have some predisposed special relationship with God, nor am I implying that Dr. Glaude believes that. Realistically, there are other outlets for personal and spiritual advancement besides the black churches' version and brand of Jesus that does not appeal to African Americans *in toto*. In essence, the black church way of doing business, in all its myriad ways is not for everyone (i.e., *all* African Americans.

The black Baptist church was not for me any longer, and if it wasn't for me, then it couldn't, by and large, be the most viable spiritual/ social platform for all African Americans. We were African American. We attend churches. However, the ways in which each church was run, the hierarchy within each church, and the end game for each church were remarkably different. The black church as I understood it to be had died. It was no longer the only game in town available to African Americans in their continuing fight for social justice, equality, and surely not economic empowerment.

That church had long since died, but I was unsure of what died first: our collective commitment or the black church itself, because there was no one to tell them to stay the course and ignore the short game.

To bring my argument into perspective, I thought about my alma mater, Grambling State University, integration of the National Football League, and historically black colleges and universities, or HBCUs.

Grambling State University is a historically black university in northwestern Louisiana. I am a proud alumnus of that college. During the '50s and several decades thereafter, this university became a haven for those African American athletes who were not allowed to go to other, traditionally white, universities solely because of the color of their skins.

Grambling State University became an incubator for the NFL as the chains of segregation were loosened. Football players such as Doug Williams, who could not even get a second look at their counterparts, therefore encouraged other similarly situated athletes to follow in their footsteps and by necessity and desire attend a historically black college or university. Grambling had no shortage of top black football talent.

However, in our zeal to collectively address the issue of desegregation, and upon the successful litigation on *Brown v. Board of Education,*[69] all schools were free to admit other races, at this time blacks, into their public educational institutions, specifically their athletic programs.

Now although the effect of segregation was to cast off the vestiges of slavery and Jim Crow and thereby give black Americans an equal chance to advance, this incubator of black athletic talent began to lose the abundance of athletic talent to larger, more financially adept, and resource-laden counterparts.

The remainder is a college that is struggling to compete with

---

[69] Brown v. Board of Education of Topeka, KS et al, 347 US 483 (1954).

these more firmly established (i.e., financially richer) entities at recruiting its fair share of athletic talent, to the chagrin of Grambling State University. The very goal sought and attained by the civil rights movement in black America had now served to somewhat diminish the long-held status of Grambling State University and a few more HBCUs as NFL incubators. This issue is relegated to athletics, but I hope you get the gist of how this applies to the black church.

The very thing sought after was attained, and the instruments or institutions that were constructed to combat and at least allow us as a people to exist and make better lives for ourselves had arguably lost its existence. But it's all in how you look at it. Every single athlete recruited at Grambling State or another HBCU was not always destined for the NFL. Things happen along the way. Does that mean the institution is no longer viable? If we were looking at Grambling State just for the purposes of recruitment of NFL talent, it's questionable.

The viability of the institution lies not only in its cash cow—the recruitment, acquisition, and promulgation of football talent—but also as a haven for those in other disciplines such as the sciences and arts who for one reason or another were rejected by other public institutions. The question with the black church is how to remain viable with the plethora of other options available.

Unless the black church returns to the social justice roots that supported and birthed its impetus, and intelligently advocates sustainability within an entirely new paradigm, it cannot remain viable.

8

ROUTINIZATION OF BLACK PROPHETIC WITNESS

Can't Continue to Live in the Past

Dr. Glaude's third and final point for the demise of the black church is the most explicit. Dr. Glaude states that "too often the prophetic energies of black churches are represented as something inherent to the institution, and we need only point to past deeds for evidence of this fact."[70] He adds, "A backward glance defines the content of the church's stance in the present—justifying its continued relevance and authorizing its voice. Its task, because it has become alienated from the moment in which it lives, is to make us venerate and conform to it."[71]

---

70 Glaude "The Black Church," pg. 2

71 Ibid.

To show how varied the black church had become, I decided to conduct an informal survey. In November 2010, I sent a survey out to approximately 117 predominantly black churches that attended the National Baptist Convention meeting Kansas City, Missouri, September 6–10, 2010. The theme of the conference was "City after God's Heart," and its program booklet included the title "Solidarity with the Savior."

At that time, I had broken ties with the black church and was questioning its moral and spiritual compass and its relevance to black lives in general. The booklet was filled cover to cover with color photographs of pastors and their wives or the buildings the members held church in, as well as pages from local sponsors such as Sprint and churches from Nebraska, Kansas, Missouri, Colorado, and other well-wishers. There was even an advertisement for a clothing store owner in Kansas City.

I only received about eighteen of the surveys back. The questions from the survey are printed out in the following pages.

SURVEY

Carefully read each question and then check the box that best approximates your response.

---

1. Please check the box that describes the average age of your church's membership:

   ❐ 0–5

   ❐ 5–12

   ❐ 12–17

   ❐ 17–25

   ❐ 25–67

   ❐ 67+

2. What is the size of your church congregation?

   ❐ 10–25

   ❐ 25–50

- ❒ 50–100
- ❒ 100–300
- ❒ 300–600
- ❒ 600–1,500
- ❒ 1,500–5,000
- ❒ 5,000+

3. If known, please describe the average level of education of the members of your church:

- ❒ No formal education
- ❒ High school diploma / GED
- ❒ Four years of college
- ❒ Master's degree
- ❒ Doctorate degree

4. What is the average monthly amount of money received from tithes to your church?

- ❒ $0.00–$5,000
- ❒ $5,000–$10,000
- ❒ $10,000–$20,000
- ❒ $25,000–$50,000
- ❒ $50,000+

5. What is the average monthly amount of money received from offerings to your church?

    - ❑ $0.00–$5,000
    - ❑ $5,000–$10,000
    - ❑ $10,000–$20,000
    - ❑ $25,000–$50,000
    - ❑ $50,000+

6. What is the average monthly amount of money received from gifts, endowments, or private donations or grants to your church?

    - ❑ $0.00–$5,000
    - ❑ $5,000–$10,000
    - ❑ $10,000–$20,000
    - ❑ $25,000–$50,000
    - ❑ $50,000+

7. How many ministries does your church have?

    - ❑ 1–10
    - ❑ 10–25
    - ❑ 25–50
    - ❑ 50–100
    - ❑ 100+

8. How many of the members on your active church roster are active in a ministry at your church?

   ☐ 10%–25%

   ☐ 25%–50%

   ☐ 50%–75%

   ☐ 100%

9. If you have an evangelism ministry at your church, what percentage of the members are active in that ministry?

   ☐ 1–10

   ☐ 10–25

   ☐ 25–50

   ☐ 50–100

   ☐ 100+

10. What amount of monthly income derived from any source your church receives does your church use toward community relief (e.g., feeding the homeless, feeding the poor, voter registration, bereaved family donations, legal fees)?

    ☐ 0–10%

    ☐ 10%–25%

    ☐ 25%–50%

    ☐ 50% or above

11. How many community outreach programs does your church have that are *not* exclusively for members of your congregation or denomination? (Examples: tutoring, economic empowerment tools, youth mentors, suicide prevention, divorce counseling.)

    none

    - ☐ 1–10
    - ☐ 10–25
    - ☐ 25 and up

12. Is either the pastor or members of your local church denomination also members of a local, national, or international Christian organization such as the National Baptist Convention?

    - ☐ Yes
    - ☐ No

13. If the answer to the question is yes, what programs have been implemented by the larger organization(s) that have positively affected the community in which you live? Please complete your answer in the space provided. Add additional sheets if necessary to complete your answer.

    ____

    ____

    ____

14. Is your pastor's position full time or part time?

- ❒ Full time
- ❒ Part time

15. What is your pastor's current yearly salary? (This means a salary paid by the congregation, the church at which the pastor provides services, not any external sources of income.)

- ❒ None
- ❒ < $10,000
- ❒ $10,000–$25,000
- ❒ $25,000–$50,000
- ❒ $50,000–$75,000
- ❒ $75,000–$100,000
- ❒ $100,000+

16. If your pastor does receive a salary from the church, is the amount common knowledge among the members of your church?

- ❒ Yes
- ❒ No

If your response if no, please state the reason(s) why in the space provided:

____

____

17. What is the highest level of education completed by your pastor?

    ☐ No formal education

    ☐ High school diploma / GED

    ☐ Four years of college

    ☐ Master's degree

    ☐ Doctorate

18. If your pastor has attained a degree or degrees higher than a high school diploma, please state the degree(s) and the area(s) of discipline in the space provided below:

____

____

____

19. Does your church financially contribute to the continuing education of the pastor?

    ☐ Yes

    ☐ No

20. Does your church financially contribute to the continuing education of the associate ministers?

    ☐ Yes

    ☐ No

21. Has your church openly affiliated with other denominations of the same faith regarding issues that affect *your* community such as youth mentoring, education reform, political reform, or crime?

❒ Yes

❒ No

22. Has your church openly affiliated with other churches NOT of your denomination regarding issues that affect *your* community such as youth mentoring, education reform, political reform, or crime?

❒ Yes

❒ No

23. Has your church pastor, laity, or representatives openly done any projects in your community toward social issues such as education, health care, taxes, affordable housing, transportation, or jobs?

❒ Yes

❒ No

If yes, please describe in the space provided below. Use additional sheets as necessary:

____

____

24. Does your pastor direct your church to openly participate in your local government in issues that affect your community such as land use, property taxes, taxation (in general), elder care, education, and the retention of public officials?

- ☐ Yes
- ☐ No

If yes, please describe what active projects your church has started or actively participated in within your community within the past four (4) years:

____

____

____

25. In the next decade, what expectations do **you** have of the church that you pastor? Please check all that apply:

- ☐ Bigger building and assets (of the church)
- ☐ Increased membership
- ☐ More community outreach
- ☐ Interdenominational outreach
- ☐ Increased study of the Bible (other languages, trip to Israel, missionary work)
- ☐ Other: ______________________________________

____

____

26. Do you believe that the black church should be solely focused on evangelizing and spiritual salvation?

❒ Yes

❒ No

27. Do you believe that the black church should be focused solely on community-based issues such as home ownership, unemployment, politics, finances, wealth accumulation, and other forms of social activism?

❒ Yes

❒ No

28. Do you believe that today's black churches have become too insulated and centralized (i.e., only committed to its own members needs and not the community-at-large, despite denomination or ethnicity?

❒ Yes

❒ No

29. Do you believe that the present-day black church has overstepped its principal biblical purpose of proclaiming the good news to the world and evolved into a business (e.g., acquiring wealth, assets, creating jobs for community/members?

☐ Yes

☐ No

30. Do you believe that the present-day black church is separated more by race or by class (local economic standing)?

☐ Yes

☐ No

The answers to these questions from the eighteen churches that did respond were as varied as the Christianity in the United States. From the results, I have been able to ascertain the following data. For the most part, the churches that did respond, responded as I believed they would. My questions were more directed to the secular, the material, the pragmatic world in which we all exist. Money, status, ministry, and education were the basis for many of the questions.

In my experience, questions about the pastor and the inner workings of the church from nonmembers were taboo. Anything that had nothing to do with service, the choir, or the ministries was forbidden to be asked and was never answered. Even members had difficult times obtaining answers from their host churches, specifically in the matters of church finance.

Many of us know that questions about money, religion, and politics are hot-button issues among humanity.

But it is absolute *anathema* to ask any church member about money, especially the pastor's salary! It's just forbidden. However, I am an outlaw.

I will start with the pastor (who is apparently the most important member of the black church, and according to all of them, in God's eyes). Again, a disappointing but respectful eighteen churches responded to the one hundred surveys I sent out.

Pastors Are Getting Degreed Up!

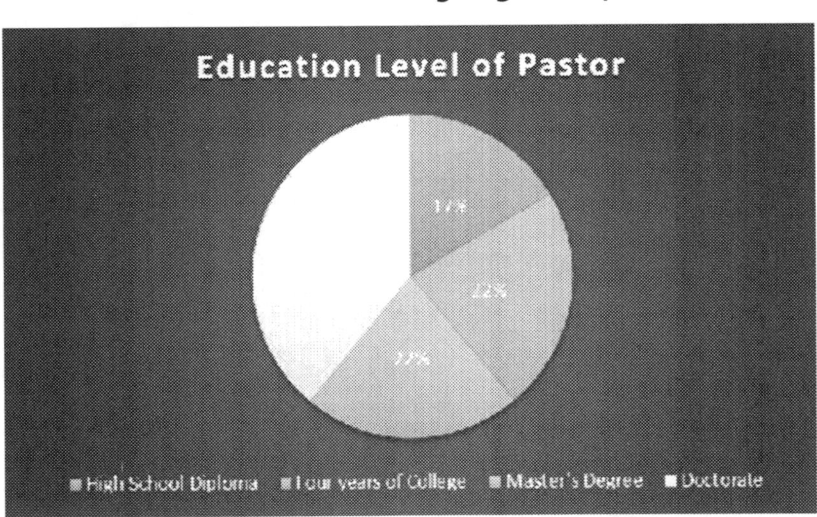

That's right. According to the surveys I received, a whopping 39 percent reported that the pastors had received doctorates. However, the survey neither asked, nor did those who answered the survey describe, in what discipline the pastors received their degrees.

There are a number of degrees a person could obtain in religious studies—religion, hermeneutics, history, theology, even a foreign language such as Greek or Hebrew that would be relevant to Christianity—but what good is it?

The Bible is replete with passages that state that God is unknowable to us.[72] The Bible even tells of how God punished man's arrogance to be "like him" in building a tower of Babel, and God, in fear or in order to teach a lesson in humility to the denizens of the earth, confounded their language, therefore disrupting their plans.[73] Furthermore, how can one man tell another man about God? It's a classic case of the blind leading the blind.[74]

I even know pastors who have degrees in other disciplines, such as psychology, business, even English or history. There is a scripture in the Bible that states God calls you {to serve} and God equips those he calls.

There is no scriptural equivalent in the Bible that states that a man should be educated to be pastor. First Timothy gives the qualifications of a pastor.[75] Absolutely none of the qualifications in the Good Book state that a pastor has to be educated or show an advanced degree in a

---

[72] Isa. 55:8 (KJV).

[73] Gen. 11:1–9 (KJV).

[74] Matt. 15:14 (KJV).

[75] 1 Tim. 3:1–7 (KJV).

particular discipline. There are no scriptural qualifications of possessing a degree from a college or university in a certain field to being a pastor and for that matter, a deacon, or anyone in possession of a spiritual gift from God. It's no different than running for student government or public office. It's all in who you know. It's about the church, which is comprised of people making an informed decision based on what someone says about a particular person, and if that person is a believer and a fiery speaker and has the power to inspire others to action.

There is nothing supernatural about it. If anything, according to the example set by Jesus, the pastor is a servant, without pride or ego, and washes the feet of his subjects, his disciples.[76]

Twenty-first-century black church pastors are more concerned now with being preeminent businessmen. The churches have become franchisee to the idea of Jesus and left to their own devices have to balance the bottom line in addition to preaching, teaching, and bringing the lost to Christ.

The nontaxable contributions of church members have bestowed working capital upon these modern-day pastors to build bigger churches, patronages, and other amenities the pastor and his family enjoy as fruits from their labors within the black church.

I am a bit impressed by the openness of pastors to enjoy their suits, jewelry, housing accommodations, continuing education, traveling

---

76 John 13:1–16 (KJV).

the country, even the world for speaking engagements and meetings with prominent businessmen, moguls supposedly first and foremost to proclaim the gospel of Christ to them. If you are doing the work of Christ, why be ashamed of the all the material wealth you have accumulated through the donations of your membership?

These full-time ministers should not be ashamed or even remotely defense or even voice justification if what they do in the name of Christ results in lavish material items such as suites, homes, cars, jewelry and most importantly, personal brand marketing. Obviously, God wants to enlarge *your* territory, right?

As bad as this economy has become, and with the scarcity of jobs, and especially in black businesses, is it any wonder that the church, with its pastors and their vision, can afford to employ other ministers, musicians, and business managers, and even private security, for the church?

If this is the case, then why doesn't the black church employ everyone who works for the church, allegedly in service to God but in reality to the church business entity? The single-parent choir member can surely use some extra money. The mass choir members who must live on fixed incomes can surely use a bit of extra money for their services. The ushers, deacons, anyone who willingly participates on a ministry in a church, should be getting some type of compensation.

The black church is easily one of the single most profitable money-making enterprises in modern America. Many churches own properties, own banks, and own recording studios, and can afford to pay the salaries of their pastors. The following is a breakdown of the tithes, offerings, and donations as provided by those eighteen churches that responded to my survey:

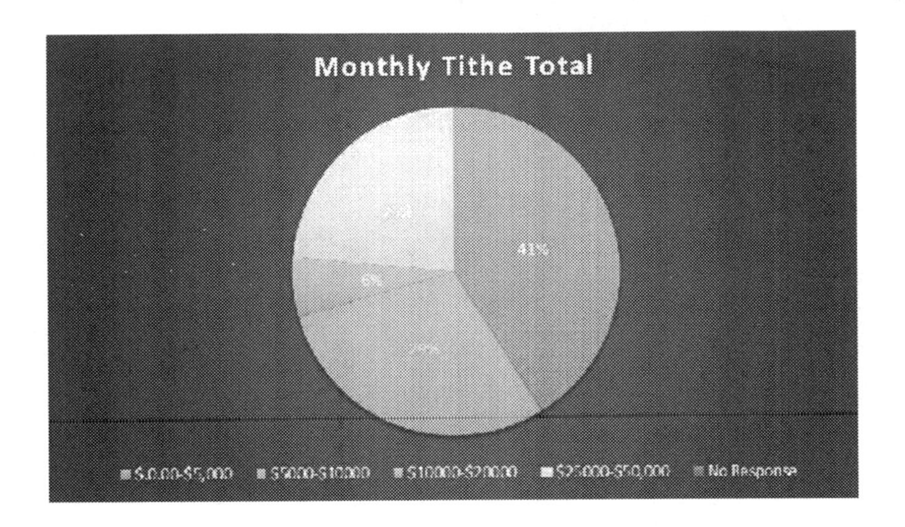

As you can see, a whopping 41 percent of those surveyed admitted to taking in at least $5,000 a month. This is easily $60,000 a year, tax-free income, without taking into account utilities and pastors' salary. Almost a third of the churches that reported admitted to taking in as much as $5,000 to $10,000 tax-free money every month, which equates to $120,000 in tithes. Alone.

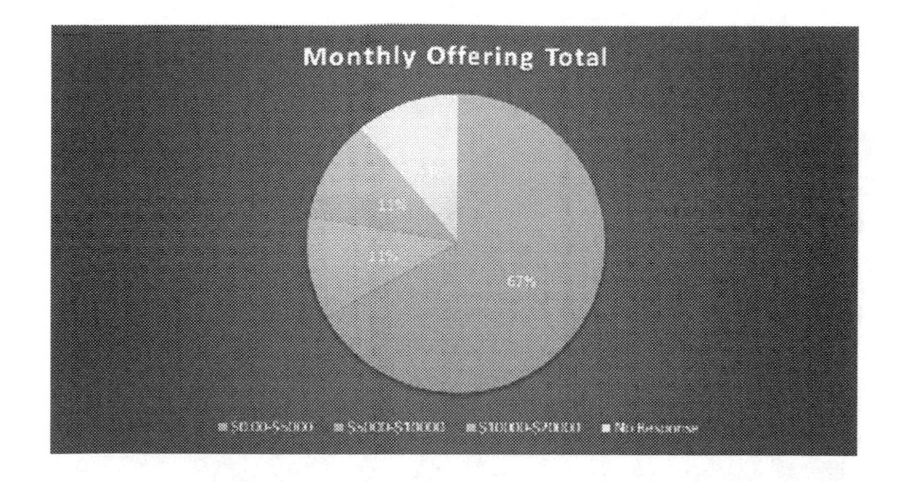

This graph depicts the churches' responses to monthly offering, which were an average $5,000 per month, again a $60,000 a year surplus of tax-free money—the maximum mean average of $5,000 per month for the average churches that reported.

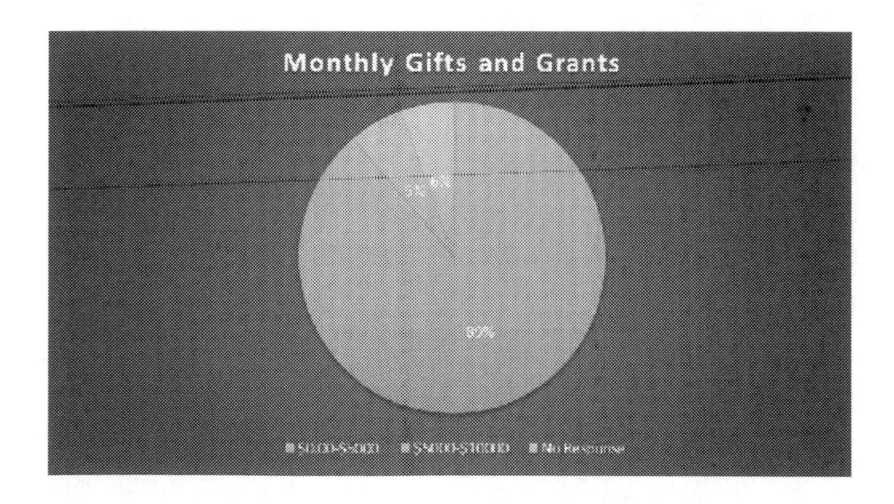

Finally, the majority of the churches reported monthly gifts and grants from outside sources in the average amount of $5,000 per month, or $60,000 per year.

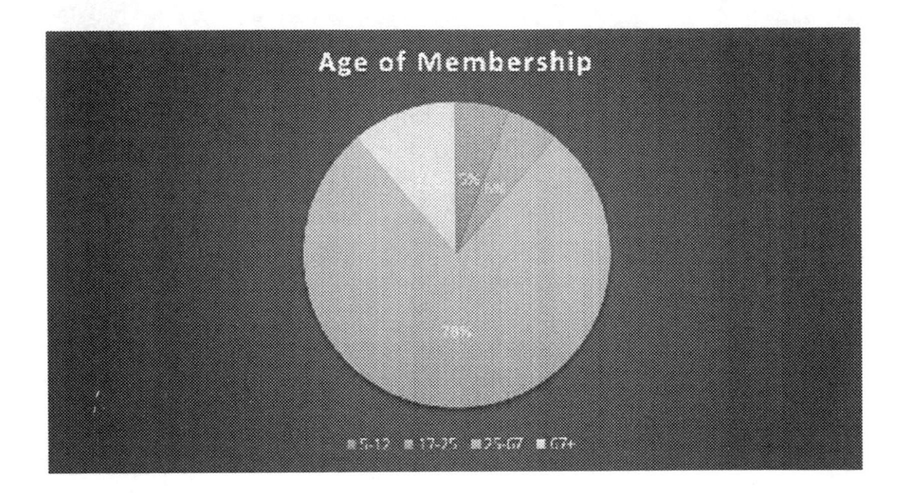

Considering that the majority of the churches surveyed reported the age of their membership were adults ages seventeen to sixty-seven,

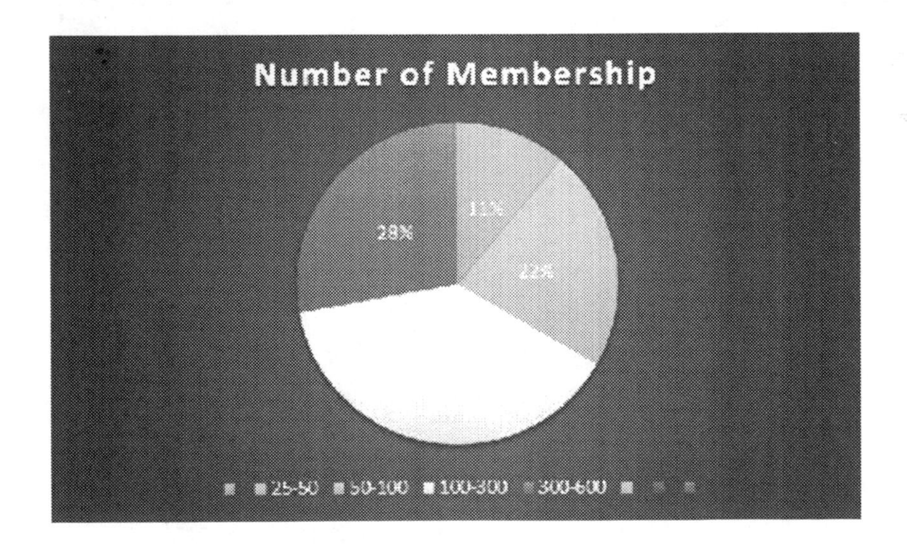

and the membership of these black churches were majority between one hundred and three hundred members,

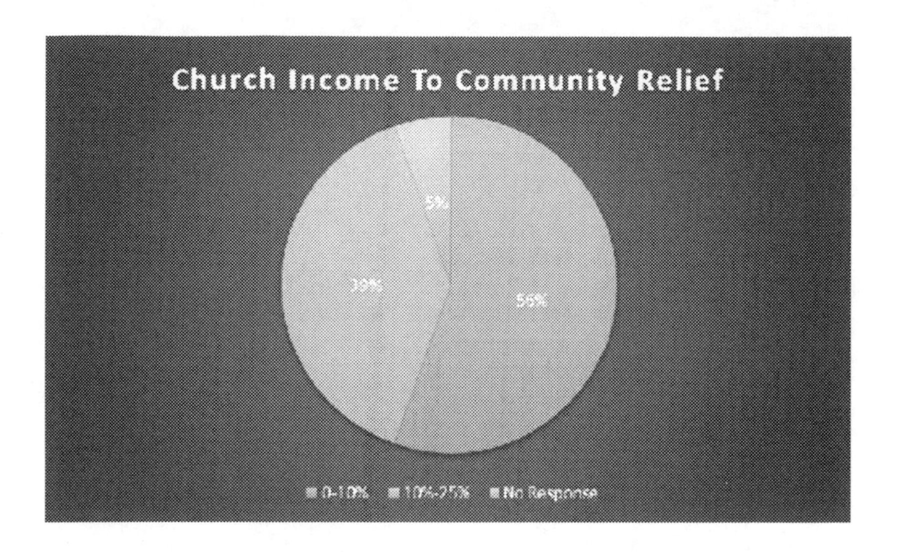

no greater than 10 percent of this church income went toward community relief projects, such as feeding the poor or providing fans to the elderly and shut-ins or other services to needy families (benevolence), the data I have accrued shows that the black church is comprised of mostly working-age young adults and adults, and from tithes, offerings, and gifts, the profit the church receives is well over $120,000 per year of tax-free income, with approximately $12,000 (roughly $1,000 per month) going to the relief of the poor.

This leaves the remaining amount of $100,000, with roughly half going toward the salary of the pastor:

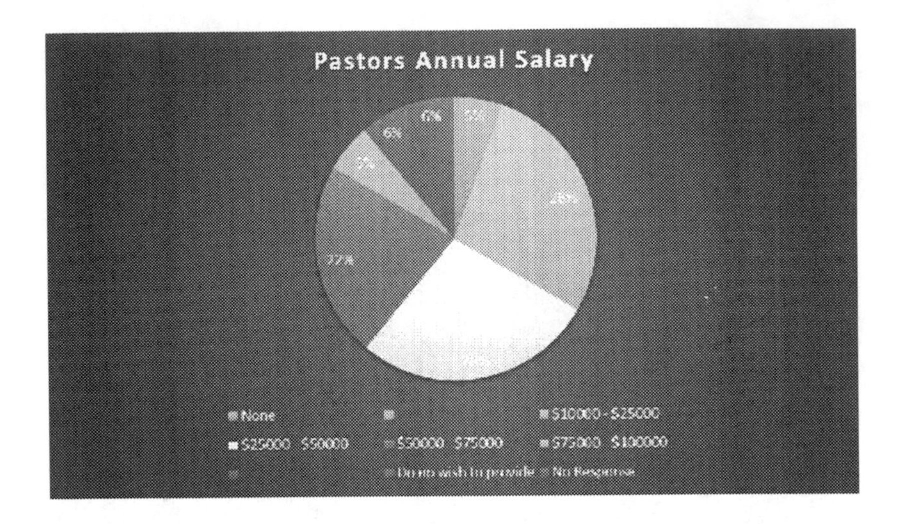

This leaves a net profit of $50,000 per year, not to include any investments that the church has made in its coffers. So it's no wonder that that coupling of investments with tithes can also increase the profit of the churches. Furthermore, the churches can also participate in commerce in such a way that they can be further blessed by God by increasing their stores.

What more viable economic business is more prevalent in the black community than the black church?

The guilt that the pastors can convey to the members and other inquisitive people can be deflected to the "tools of the enemy" attempting to tear down this black institution.

As far as payment is concerned, there is only one verse that specifically states that the priests should earn a living from the ministry.[77] There is another verse I have heard quoted by pastors and preachers justifying pay for their services in the form of "taking your hand from the plow."[78]

Pastors have earned their spot in the black church due to their alleged humility in servitude and care for the personal issues of their own members and the Christian counseling they give to others. The common duties of pastors are preaching on Sunday mornings and afternoons (where applicable), visiting the sick, visiting and performing the Communion for the elderly shut-in, officiating marriages and funerals and leading Bible study.

However, in modern American society, the black pastor is seen as a leader in the black community, especially if the pastor is well liked and his church is well stocked with tithe-paying obedient members. Our counterparts attribute some type of mind control phenomena over these particular zealots. And the zealots know it. The zealots believe it. Their cult of personality, the popularity of the pastors and the high number of their followers, almost guarantees that they will be sought out by their counterparts because they have shown they have the power of persuasion.

Their style and panache speak to the masses, and therefore continue to exert control over certain members of the black community that

---

[77] 1 Cor. 9:14 "do the work of the ministry, ought to be able to live off the ministry" (KJV).

[78] 1 Tim. 5:18: "Do not muzzle an ox while it is treading out the grain" (KJV).

would otherwise be impossible to attain. The pastor as businessman and entrepreneur also muddies the waters as the prosperity gospel approach has been criticized as early as the mid-1990s. This prosperity gospel is preached predominantly by Creflo Dollar, who recently did a Kickstarter campaign of sorts for a new jet for ministry purposes.

The pastor as pimp is a common theme in black churches, particularly in the black community. The pastor is answerable to no one but God.[79] The majority of those outside the church, and even those within it, have always had an issue with the money the church takes in, and the pastors showcasing new cars, suits, and other material wealth while the members, the community across the street from the church, is made all the worse.

My grandfather, God rest his soul, exposed me to this truism early on. He never attended church, and his justification was that the "pastor was a crook," and the pastor wanted complete obedience from all of his members while he got to operate in complete autonomy, again, only beholden to the dictates of the God the rest of us could not see. The parishioners cannot trust their own judgment because the pastor has created the illusion of the literal appearance of sovereignty, answerable to no one, not even the US government, because of the

---

[79] James 3:1 (KJV).

church's 501(c)(3) compliance,[80] and additionally the protections of the First Amendment of the US Constitution.[81]

It's like an open secret. Those who attend church wonder what makes the pastor so much better than them that he gets to make money, and operate with impunity and without question in the "name of Jesus," while they suffer and scrape by, and if they miss church service or it has been conveyed to the pastor that they are sinning against God, this pastor can judge them and recite Scripture against them. Moreover, someone who does not tithe or have a "church home" or does not attend afternoon church service, or donate a bit extra at the pastor's behest, will not receive a blessing from God.

While the parishioner or burgeoning believer awaits a blessing from God, the pastor is still seen as a living breathing godhead.

The transparency that needs to occur within the black church is one in which the quasimystical power that prevents the public or members from questioning the pastor, or being led to follow blindly the dictates of a man who claims God is speaking to him and him only,

---

80 Portion of the US tax code that allows for federal tax exemption of nonprofit organizations, especially those that are considered public charities, private foundations, or private operating foundations US tax code that makes churches nontaxable entities under US law.

81 "Congress shall make no law respecting an establishment of religion, or prohibiting the free exercise thereof." United States Constitution, Section 1, Amend. 1.

and the biggest lie, that if you don't financially give money to God or show faithfulness to the church, you will be cut off from God and be cursed forever.

This rhetoric no longer has sway over a number of people. What makes the average person of color so unloved by God because of his or her nonaffiliation with the black church? The black church is not a religious institution. The black church is not solely an evangelizing institution. Today's black church is still trying to define itself under the old mystique of community activist and organizer, which is no longer the case. The black church lacks transparency because it tries to be all things to all black people, and there is no clear directive to the people of God, no unanimity among the believers, only the dictates of the pastor and those who adhere to what they believe are the pastor's directions and actions as crudely supported by scripture.

Two questions in the survey asked what the church's sole (primary) responsibility was in the community, and neither response was conclusive. A majority of those surveyed stated that evangelism was not the sole mission of the church, nor was community outreach.

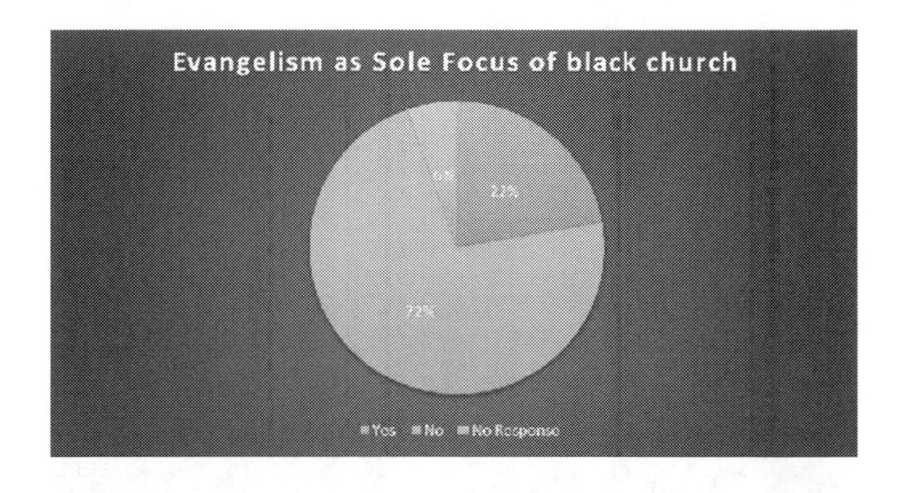

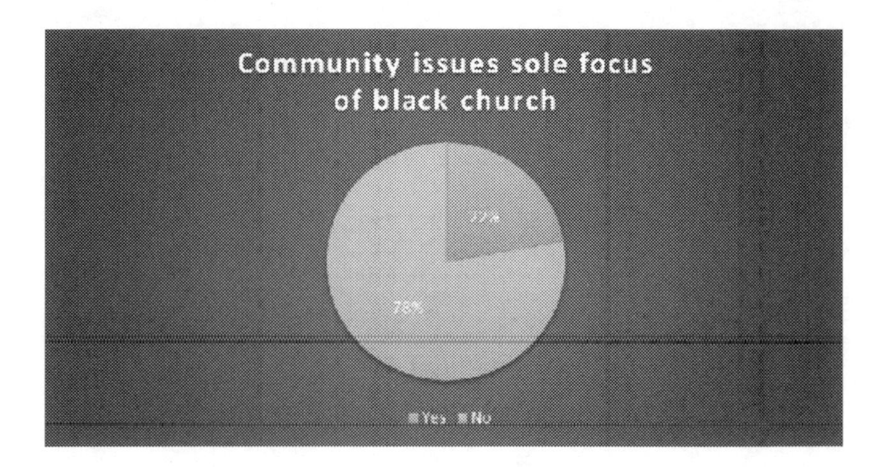

There is clearly a lack of accountability within the black church. There is no clear-cut direction except for what the pastor instructs the individual congregants to do or missions to perform. This final point is supported by the next graph:

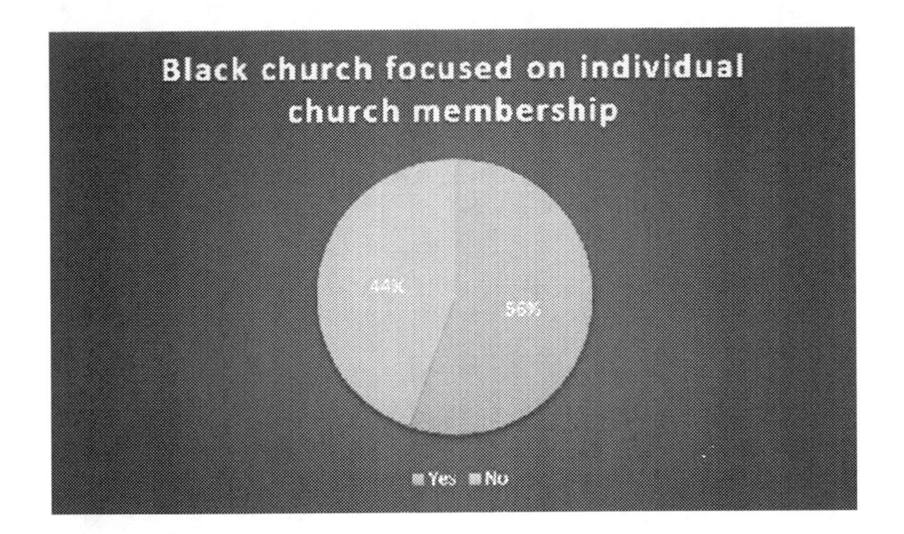

The majority of those who responded asserted that the black church is focused on the needs and dictates of individual church membership, whatever those relevant needs may be.

OF OUR NEW DAY BEGUN

THE NEW PARADIGM

There can simply be no black church, as there are too many individuals with agendas. The commonality of purpose that Jesus stated to the disciples was threefold: proselytize,[82] feed the sheep,[83] and love one another.[84]

---

[82] Matt. 28:19 (KJV).

[83] John 21:15–17 (KJV).

[84] John 13:34–35 (KJV).

We know the code of conduct from the Bible. We know what we should receive from one another and how we should treat one another, but the dictates and results and mission as applied by and through the pastor or whatever form of "church leadership" you ascribe to are as varied as the denominations of Christianity itself.

If the black church cannot admit to this lack of commonality and become more transparent to today's educated persons instead of relying on antiquated traditions and supernatural rhetoric, it will be continue to exist in its own fiction, devoid of power and reduced to nothing but a vacuous title of bygone days. Own what you are and move forward. If you operate the church as a business, be a business, but don't try to punish or condemn those who question your existence or your integrity. By their fruit ye shall know them.[85]

There are plenty of nonreligious entities that the black church can and should morph into to remain relevant in today's society. The black church has always had its underpinnings in religion, in its fervent desire to continue a social gospel as inspired by Jesus Christ.

However, today's black church has opened my eyes to something even more prevalent: faith is free, but religion will cost you.

To me, eliminating the name "church" from the title is a great start. The words "center," "fellowship," "life center," "house of prayer," are all acceptable changes. The term "black church" denotes a series of

---

85 Matt. 7:15–20 (KJV).

practices and operations that are apparently justified in doing the will of God here on earth. Furthermore, the connotation is that the black church is the family, the pure, primal place where people of color must congregate and be subjected to and governed by the will and dictates of the pastor *as passed by and ordained by God*, so they will stay honest and true to themselves, their pastor, their church, their church family, and those who do not know Christ, so they can show themselves worthy when Jesus Christ returns to judge whether they are worthy of entry into heaven.

The individual black churches are havens of hypocrisy and judgment, and no one, no one, has the courage of conviction to judge the pastor lest he or she face ostracism or banishment from the "church family."

This is not the type of governance that a religion dictates. The Bible commands us to preach and teach the gospel to the world, and to go after the lost sheep,[86] those who leave the congregation for unknown reasons because Jesus wants the one lost sheep the most. This is where the "black church" fails to be a haven for the lost and wicked and rejected, and falls short in its ministry. This is where the black church disintegrates into a nonreligious entity. It cannot be holy because its people are not holy. Learn to accept where you are, and call yourself what you are. The church is a nonreligious entity. As the

---

86 Luke 15:1–7, Matt. 18:12 (KJV).

Bible preaches, Jesus came to save us because we could not keep all the commandments of his Father. Not one.

The reality is that the black church is no longer a beacon to guide the lost but has become a money-making enterprise. The church is a powerful nonprofit entity where only a few can partake of the financial blessings, and only a few, I might add, while the remainder work with the hopes that their unquestioning commitment would give them a greater reward in heaven.

I can recall when discussing a matter of the Bible in church in Bible study how the participants' faces would change when you brought up something that challenged the teacher or the pastor based on science or another generally accepted tome, or even a nugget of wisdom that wasn't "spiritually derived" from the Bible.

The black church may have had its origins in pain, misery and assimilation, but it was not destined to be the only way to a better life, a better way to understand Christ and fulfill your destiny. Black America was on the move educationally, vocationally, and, as a result, spiritually.

Statistics show that dropout rates declined faster among blacks ages eighteen to twenty-four. Poverty rates among blacks have declined over time to 27 percent, down from 31.3 percent in 1976.[87]

---

[87] Jens Manuel Krogstad, *Six Facts About Black Americans for Black History Month* (Pew Research Center, 2015).

Additionally, 4.5 million African Americans had obtained a four-year degree from a college or university.[88]

These statistics show for better or for ill that black America is educating itself and attempting to move across social strata to a more comfortable way of life. This comfortable way of life may not include disavowing organized religion as a whole, but I believe that it has forced black Americans to open their eyes and realize that their opportunities are not by and large dictated or driven by their membership in a black church.

If anything, the more educated a person becomes, the more he or she begins to see the abuses and judgmental attitudes and actions of members of the church and seeks to go elsewhere, where like-minded individuals can freely question the pastor, yea, even the scriptures themselves.

I have always felt that the black church at one time detested some forms of education, particularly those disciplines such as philosophy and science that sought to question the pastor on things said or done during and between services.

These people of color who did wholeheartedly agree with the scripture were ostracized. Those who sought counsel with the pastor about their beliefs were immediately told to go and pray for guidance but to never question the pastor publicly again for fear of upsetting the congregation.

---

88 *Journal of Blacks in Higher Education.*

In this changing world, I had become a liberal spiritualist because the Bible as applied in the black churches I had attended and in the entertainment-fest known as gospel music, and the "do what I say or you won't get blessed" rhetoric of black churches died out. At the conclusion of my expansion on this point of Dr. Glade's, I can only say with extreme confidence to other African Americans this one thing: I know I am not the only one who feels this way.

Dr. Glaude's final statements regarding the death knell of the black church, and his self-described most important one, was the routinization of black prophetic witness. He states "The prophetic energies of the black churches are represented as something inherent to the institution."[89]

Glade poignantly illustrates statements such as, "The black church has always stood for ...," or "The black church was our rock," or "Without the black church, we would not have ..." that are uttered by those of a bygone generation that did not attempt to evolve the church into the present to address the changing social, educational, economic, and spiritual issues that pervade our community.

When the church was viable in the black community, it was a place to sound off about what ailed you. The black church was commensurate to a speakeasy where not only were frustrations vented; actions and

---

[89] Glaude, "The Black Church," 3.

aspirations were actualized in the form of marches and community gatherings at the courthouses and legislative buildings in the cities.

In those days, not only did the pastor go out, but the members all marched or had the same common cause, and, dare I say, belief in God.

As the Bible states: "He whom the son sets free is free indeed."[90]

Dr. Glaude summarizes in the final lines of his paper that the black church can no longer live on its past successes. The black church should be respected for its place in history, but history is meant to looked upon as a reference so our present actions do not repeat the same missteps of our past but the black church must become something greater than its storied past.

I believe that a day is coming when the system that has been carefully constructed by pastors and preachers who built up edifices will be replaced by using the finances and resources of the church to build up people individually and then build up the community in which they exist.

I believe a day is coming where those who put money in the church coffers to pay bills of the church and salaries of the pastor and the employees of the church (employees of the church?) can and will be put to use within the community in which those churches exist.

I was viewing *Black in America: Almighty Debt*, a special that

---

[90] John 8:36 (KJV).

appeared on CNN helmed by Ms. Soledad O'Brien in October 2010 with my wife, and the question arose about the original intent of the church. We also queried each other about what the church should be doing with this particular crisis. The answer was quickly provided: to save souls, to bring nonbelievers into the fold, and to go out and convert other nonbelievers to living a life in Jesus Christ.

I was wondering whether the ills that plague many African Americans are wrought or even exacerbated by this belief in giving tithes to an institution that does not give immediate benefits when you have bills due, and you are trying to make ends meet, whether you made bad decisions about managing money or if you were the unwitting victim in this economic downturn.

Soledad O'Brien posed the question to T. D. Jakes and Pastor DeForest Soaries of whether God favors you materially by your faith.[91] Soaries stated the church helps "if you preach prosperity, there will be a gap ... it's an ecclesiastical pyramid scheme where the preacher gets rich and the people get tricked" ... to "create big dreams and provide infrastructure to deal with your newfound faith-based success."

Does God provide materially for the faithful? Jakes totally sidestepped the question by replying it is "faith and works" ... that the theology is flawed because of those who are abusing it blatantly.

When I arrived in Kansas City, Missouri, in 1999, I became a

---

91 *God in America: Almighty Debt*, CNN, October 23, 2010.

member of a church that many ascribed as "being on the move," and whose people were warm and loving and nonjudgmental. Those who were patrons of this congregation were also described as Christlike and had Christlike attitudes and mannerisms.

It seemed like a dream come true, and, as with most people, it was a utopia to me, a virtual heaven on earth.

But what eventually happens once you become indoctrinated with a culture is that the leader or leaders in the church begin to show who they really are. The black church is probably the biggest minority-owned corporation ever created. Its membership, board of directors, and community relations board is comprised mainly of those people who believe in a cause and condition greater than themselves: *Jesus Christ*. They believe their mission is to live out the wishes and desires of the God they serve by being able to instruct and mold those believers who come to the church for spiritual guidance into the common lives of those who live outside the church.

Now the motive, like the true message of Christ, love, is great in theory. However, the dissension lies in the application of the theory, the process that the pastors and parishioners use to convey this message. For my purposes, I will only deal with the black church.

1. The Diversity in Black Church Membership

The members who are a part of the church are convinced that the principles of Jesus Christ are being lived by those who are members, based on their appearance and their speech patterns. They appear to be loving and giving and prayerful. The longer you are around these people, these "church folk" as I have designated them, you see that are more judgmental and less transparent than those sinners whom they are trying to convince to join their church.

The average age of these members, the most dedicated, is past fifty years of age. For the most part, this becomes readily acceptable because the parishioners are not taught to dwell on the settings of the scriptures. They were derived from cultures where women were to be loved as God loves humanity or as a human being could love another human being. However, the one difference was that women had no place in politics or leadership in any facet of existence.

Therefore, you would see a mass of men in leadership positions in the church, and positions that women were appointed to were servile in nature, no true power or influence over those whom they were given assignment over.

A recent development has been an increase of women pastors and preachers in many black denominations. These changes may have been politically motivated or may be merely a literal reading of the Bible in the administration of spiritual gifts among people. In the books of Corinthians and Thessalonians, there are no gender limitations on the gifts of the spirit.[92]

However, it could merely be a reflection of what the casual

---

[92] 1 Cor. 1:1–11; Eph. 4:11–14.(KJV)

observer of a typical church would see: approximately 75 percent of the attendees are female, mostly single mothers.[93]

Millennials want Jesus. I believe that. They are human. They want to believe in something greater than themselves, something that can give them hope to go on in the presence of cruelty and hypocrisy walking alongside their fellow man.

Millennials don't want to access Jesus the same way we did, the way our parents and grandparents and great-grandparents continue to do: by exercising judgment and condemnation against nonbelievers and all those who don't speak, dress, and act in piety toward Jesus Christ. They want worship without commitment or critique from a figurehead that is just as human and fallible as they themselves are.

At forty-two years of age, however, it is becoming increasingly difficult for me to reconcile being a black American Christian with a progressive social justice mind-set. For example, the LGBTQ movement is challenging each of us, challenging how we Christians apply the principles as conveyed in the Bible as they relate to homosexual activity.

God abhors homosexuality.[94] Alternatively, Jesus Christ proposed that love is the greatest commandment. How are we as a modernist society to deal with open homosexuality when the very laws interpreted

---

93 *PEW Forum on Religion and Public Life*, 2009.

94 1 Cor. 6:9–11, Lev. 18:22, 1 Cor. 7:2, Mark 10:6–9. (KJV)

in our country prevent its citizens from treating unfairly those who are a protected class?

States, more importantly, the constituents of states, have passed and are attempting to pass "religious freedom" laws. These laws are used to circumvent what would and could be normally associated with open discrimination against those of the LGBTQ community based on the abridgment of the freedom of religion.

Basically, I can choose not to serve homosexuals because the religious convictions that I practice cannot be compelled to be conformed or violated if a particular practice is in direct contravention to my religious beliefs (i.e., homosexuality).

The blowback comes for entertainers, private businesses, big corporations, movers and shakers, and even Christians who I believe are following Jesus's words of loving each other by not hurting one another. Those who are in opposition to the religious freedoms acts may sincerely believe that tenet; for some, it may be truly brand management in that they don't want to lose any money from any customers by offending this class of protected people. I am a bit jaded and believe it's more of the latter than any genuine, absolute belief that Jesus's words should be interpreted in direct contravention to those of his Father regarding homosexuality. The LGBTQ community has flexed its muscles, and the black church, and all Christians, have bowed their heads in contrition to the marketing machine and for the sake of keeping the relative peace and not being offensive to anyone.

But the Bible the generations are seeking to teach the millennials to adhere to says very clearly to "hate what God hates and love what God loves."[95] The confusion for a Bible reader of any level is to determine whether to read the Bible as a whole or "cherry-pick" what is relevant for you and your goal.

Face it, people. This is confusing. And as long as we cannot reconcile what the Bible says to what we ought to do as believers, that will make us innovators or heretics. But all have sinned and fallen short of the glory of God.[96] Which do we enforce? The Old Testament blood-and-guts God, or the Golden-Rule-packing-love-is-the-greatest-commandment-of-all- New Testament Jesus?

If you look in terms of slavery, I guess the same question could have been proffered to those in power at the time. However, since the slaves were treated so harshly by their masters for minuscule infractions, it was only a matter of time before their slave masters could be seen to be out of step with the Holy Bible in their treatment of slaves.

A trope in the black church is that the minister of music has always been gay. There has always been a presence of homosexuality in the church, just as there were people in the church who were liars,

---

95 Ps. 97:10 (KJV)

96 Rom. 3:23.(KJV)

cheaters, coveted others' spouses, and sowed seeds of discord among the brethren, all the juicy sins that are an abomination to God.[97] So in the face of all of this hypocrisy, is the black church still an entity that is relevant and alive and spiritually advancing the cause of Christianity in black life?

I have to emphatically answer no. The black church that I grew up in at first had a very literal translation of the Bible for its members and adherents. Today's church simply has glossed over the homosexuality component but also has imploded upon itself by going against its traditions of the maintaining of office by sinful, sex-crazed, money-seeking ministers, and promoting the concept of female and homosexual female ministers.

It seems the black church cannot win for losing. To reject those people is not an act of love as described by Jesus. However, Jesus came not to destroy the law but to fulfill it.[98]

The Black Church: Recovery/Devolution

Step One: Transparency

The black church is dead. It is not in need of rescue. As I heard it said many times during my life, we are blessed by the continual prayers

---

97 Prov. 6:16–19. (KJV)

98 Matt. 5:17 (KJV).

of our mamas. It is only by grace that we are able to live in times such as these.

I believe in order for there to be a church, much less a "black" church, there must be a transparency in the way the old regime operated, and the way a new paradigm twenty-first-century church must operate. That body must devolve, I mean to say, go back to the roots of its strength and power: the power of Christ that dwells within us all. In order for there to be a church, the literal walls must be broken down, and belief in a power within yourself coupled with the honest belief and efforts of others, internal and external to you, to make God's power real in your life.

Christians are under attack more than ever, and it's mainly because of the perception that they are judgmental and hypocritical. The "militant" evangelist church, I freely admit, is one that I admire because at least they quote the scripture they believe justifies their actions, and they act with a clear purpose due to their literal interpretation of the Bible. An example is Westboro Baptist Church, out of Topeka, Kansas. Those church members will protest and come out in numbers with voices and signage quoting biblical scriptures as they believe wholeheartedly in the literal interpretation of the Bible and are not ashamed of whom they offend or how marginalized or politically incorrect or blatantly offensive they appear to be.

They have used the constitutional right to assemble as their benchmark, and their First Amendment rights to actively politic against the governmental entities they believe act in contradiction to the scriptures. The church is also predominantly white.

I only bring out this point because, for the life of me, aside from the civil rights movement and Black Lives Matter, I have never seen the black church organized to the levels of advocating God's displeasure at things unholy.

Our conversation is not about our crisis. Our message is not about our misery. Our ministries do not support a collective movement. Our power is not used for our progress.[99] These are the symptoms of a church that has outlived its usefulness because, through the efforts of our predecessors, we have basically eliminated the mission statement of those old venerated entities.

Let me illustrate.

I believe that a devolution is necessary. I am not proposing that the churches open their doors collectively and throw all of their capital in the streets and allow the public a free-for-all for the monies collected from years of frightening people to pay their tithes. The church should take a new look at the individual and at the times that the twenty-first century have produced.

Somewhere in our American odyssey, we have turned over control of our lives and destinies not only to the church, but to selected emissaries who articulate our frustrations and concerns, and tackle

---

99 Dixon, *If God Is So Good*, 139.

racial and social injustices in our name. African Americans have been conditioned to turn their personal power over to men and women who encourage them to "wait on God" or depend on external forces.[100]

We reason that since we have no power, we need to be saved by someone else.[101] There was created within the black church the means of its own destruction, the loss of our ever-loving minds and the ability to think independently from others, despite the biblical quotes and fear of ostracism.

Remember when you wanted to speak out about the pastor or a point he preached about? As if on cue, the pulpit became a huge sword and shield, and the pastor would state: "Touch not my anointed!"[102]

Remember when the tithes were low, and you had lost your job and had a newborn baby to take care of? Remember the pastor *first* implying that you would be struck dead like Aninas and Sapphira because you were conspiring to "rob God"?[103]

Remember when you had a question about the pastor's salary and what he did to earn it and how it didn't seem fair that the minister was getting an exorbitant amount of money while others in the church were truly suffering financially? The pastor would quote that the

---

[100] Burrell, *Brainwashed*, 186.

[101] Ibid., 198.

[102] 1 Chron. 16:21–22 (KJV).

[103] Mal. 3:10 (KJV).

"priest who does the work of the ministry should be able to make a living off the ministry."[104]

These are just a few examples of what I experienced as a member of the black church—the actual body. Some church organizations are now so big that self-preservation and organizational growth are their chief concerns.[105]

Tom Burrell, a marketing strategist, promotes collective obsolescence of the black church by outlining the short-term and long-term benefits of the promulgation of the black church as it was.

The short-term benefits to carrying on business as usual in the original black church paradigm are the following:

1. Religious resignation, where your destiny is totally beyond your control and is God's will for your life.
2. Suffering is your lot in life and is your way of earning reward points to heaven.
3. Your hope is fomented by the kind words of the minister and by scriptural references such as, "I have overcome the world," and "God is more than the world against us."
4. If you financially invest in your pastor, you will be blessed financially as well.

---

[104] 1 Cor. 9:13–14.

[105] Burrell, *Brainwashed*, 201.

5. Follow previously established leaders without question because they have the resources and the know-how to lead you into the marvelous light.

Long-Term Costs of Religious Obsolescence

1. Believing God has willed misfortune on you reinforces a sense of innate unworthiness and robs you of your ability to seek out your own solutions here in the tangible, pragmatic world.
2. Believing it is your lot to suffer allows you to tolerate unquestioningly and even seek suffering. Think about the self-flagellation of the monk in the movie *The DaVinci Code*.
3. Constantly seeking external avenues of hope instead of galvanizing it from within into personal action keeps you in a childlike dependent position.
4. You have just as much right to prosperity as the minister (God is not a respecter of persons) and a better chance of achieving it through your own initiative.
5. Waiting on guidance robs you of personal initiative and accountability, while reinforcing feelings of inadequacy.[106]

Burrell speaks of this as a shift in thinking to create self-appointed leaders, freethinkers of a sort. However, looking to scriptures, I use the

---

106 Burrell, *Brainwashed*, 201–4.

fact that we all have been blessed with spiritual gifts,[107] regardless of gender or financial status.

The transparency that I am speaking of is the full, unadulterated power of scripture that qualifies all of us with the individual power to change our circumstances.

The greatest test for transparency is for people to come forward, especially church folk, to tell the tale of God and the applicability of his power through people (i.e., the black church). This includes the building of believers who still remain some of the most noninclusive, judgmental, arrogant, and self-assured people I have ever met.

The way that you would hear most black church members talk, the building and its pastor and its believers have some type of quasimystical power attributed to their faithfulness to their congregation, the church they attend, and whose membership they serve.

Black churches are not very inclusive. Even with all of the rhetoric and dogma about Jesus coming to convert and save Gentiles, black churches remain one of the hardest places to join and remain in the good graces of membership and laity alike. It has been my personal experience that the more educated you are and the more you question the symbolism of the Bible, the more of a heretic and blasphemer you are.

---

[107] 1 Cor.12:7-11 (KJV).

You may or may not believe this, but pastors *hate* to tell the public, even their own members, how much money they rake in on a yearly basis.

Black Church as a Business Enterprise

As a child and young adult, I was taught to put money in the collection plate. I was made to feel ashamed by my parents and peers if I held out or did not donate money when the offering plate came around. I often wondered to myself where the money was going, but I never vocalized or asked. I was a child and did not pay bills, but I knew things cost money. The money I provided was given by my mother or grandmother before church began.

This repetition began to convince me that I had to make a financial contribution to God via the church so I could show God my appreciation for answered prayers and to fall in line with my peers. As I got older, the money that jingled was frowned upon by both the pastor and my peers, but the money that folded became a symbol of status and continued blessing and favor for my obedience to God.

From the time I began attending church to my self-imposed exile, the scriptures of reference for giving came from the story of Abraham when God called him away from his kin to establish a new nation from his progeny.[108] At first, as a new Christian, I had no problem with this because I wanted to stay in favor with God and be good and continue to have good health and food and candy and all the accoutrements that went with obedience to God. It wasn't until I got older that I started seeing a change in the social dynamic between the pastor and his constituents.

Without even knowing the pastor's financial state, it appeared that most black pastors and preachers I knew had an affluence that was rarely seen and experienced in the black community in which I lived. On Sundays, the pastor always wore multiple rings on his fingers, drove around in pricey cares and wore beautiful suits with cuff links, tiepins and ascots. And this was all from preaching the word of God.

As Booker T. Washington noted in his book *Up from Slavery*, when the colored folk were freed and sought to educate themselves, many of them either wanted to be preachers or teachers. Even as far back as the Reconstruction Period between 1867 -1878, Washington observed that although freed blacks were ravenous for education, because of the sheer number of those who were enrolled in schools throughout the region, "the idea, however, was too prevalent that, as soon as one secured a little education, and in some unexplainable way he would be

---

108 Genesis: Abraham gave a tenth of what he had on the altar as a sacrifice to God.

free from most of the hardships of the world, and, at any rate, could live without manual labour".[109]

Moreover, Washington observed that "a large portion took up teaching or preaching as an easy way to make a living".[110] Washington's most telling statement about this influx of ministers that I find relevant in the 21st century states "the ministry was the profession that suffered most...on account of not only ignorant but in many cases immoral men who claimed that they were "called to preach"". Maybe these black folks saw the authority and power these preachers possessed to rally people around them, the power through their personality to receive extra benefits because someone so gifted had to be blessed by God. And if you want to stay in God's graces, you blessed the pastor or preacher financially. Where did this line of thinking come from in black culture? The answer is fear coupled with ignorance.

The fire and brimstone sermons combined with the slaves' fidelity to their slave owners and victimist mindset contributed to the continued obedience, forgiveness and joy in spite of your impoverished condition and generally accepted disdain by society as animals or lacking the intellectual capacity to understand or reason the Bible to their own circumstances. Such an endeavor takes time and courage which I why I have undertaken this endeavor.

---

109 Washington, *Up From Slavery*, pg.66

110 Ibid.

To be fair, such ignorance and fear was not merely endemic to black people. I understand this book deals with the Black Church and I have been carrying on quite a bit about blacks but white Europeans had the same issues. During the Protestant Reformation, Martin Luther decried the practice of indulgences.[111] Priests would basically promise to talk to the Almighty on behalf of a person in exchange for money or legal tender or property of the person seeking God's forgiveness and favor. This was a common practice in Europe for hundreds of years. Martin Luther uses the same basis of faith and freedom, the latter of the two would not be grasped either literally or intellectually by black Americans for a century or more to come, to craft elegant theses to the Church about the freedom of a Christian.

As I have pointed out thus far, the lure of easy money at this point is only part of what makes those so emboldened to become pastors and preachers. Most, not all in my opinion do so for the "tax free" compensation doled out by their members.

The only reference I found that justifies any type of wage or gift to pastors originated in 1 Corinthians 9:13-14, which quotes: "Don't you know that those who work in the temple get their food from the temple, and those who serve at the altar share in what is offered on the altar? In the same way, the Lord has commanded that those who

---

111 Luther, *The Freedom of a Christian*, pg. 20-21 Fortress Press, Minnesota. See also "Ninety-five Theses, 1517," WA 1:233; LW 31:25

preach the gospel should receive their living from the gospel."[112] The scripture does not justify a certain amount, only that a wage can be paid to a priest.

The modern-day priests now live in extravagance, often forsaking employment in the private sector and becoming full-time pastors, with a few even receiving a salary in six figures. The pastors live better than the laity. They look and dress better than the laity. They are supposedly blessed more than the laity simply on the premise that they are pastors/preachers/priests and have created a cult of personality around themselves, I mean, Jesus. The black church is an old new business model for black America.

When you have a church that makes six figures a year, and over 50 percent of that goes to the pastor and 10 percent or less goes to feeding the poor and helping the homeless, where does the remaining balance go? Is it for benevolence? Oh, before I forget, most churches do pay for musicians every Sunday, pay for the services of a business manager, associate pastor(s), administrative assistants, private security, and, most times, the home or parsonage of the minister.

Where is it justified scripturally that a church is responsible for all of these amenities? Why in black churches is it necessary, and does the laity condone or agree with the exorbitance of its pastors? In the eyes

---

[112] "I Cor. 9:13-14" (NIV).

of many, depending on the oratorical skills of the pastors, they look like rock stars. What do you think the millennials think of the black church?

I think that millennials believe that the black church is nonexistent, or if it does exist, it does not have the teeth or force of its convictions to cultivate change.

As I once learned the hard way, just because you have "Negro" in the name, does not mean you qualify. As a young man who was seeking to attend college at Grambling State University, I applied to the United Negro College Fund for a scholarship to assist with paying my tuition. I completed the required essay and provided documentation about my acceptance and did everything very early, far ahead of the date of submission.

I received a response from the committee and was told that because Grambling State University was not on a list of schools for which the fund would provide educational money, I was not going to receive assistance from them. I was heartbroken. I was "united," and I was a "negro," and I was entering "college," but even then, in that instance when society had shown me negative exception because of my color, I *still* could not catch a break.

Rescue of the Black Church

Enter Black Lives Matter

Millennials will attempt to go to black churches in their communities because of their familial or neighborhood traditions and because the tradeoff is an outlet for their talents and skills. A smile from the pastor here, a handshake there, and the seeds have been sown for that person to be in the fold, counted as a statistic, someone whom the black church is assisting in this mean, cold world—a person for whom the black church is making a difference.

As these millennials get older, though, they see the church becoming bedfellows with politicians locally and abroad, apparently compromising the ideals of Christ for the stardom of the pastor or the notoriety of the church. Often, it is the pastor, not the laity or the members, who receives the recognition and the praise, and the church, *through* the pastor, that receives a gift or financial benefit.

Many young people see the church as being more involved in the funerals of its slain sons and daughters and performing prayer vigils as opposed to really doing something about the issues that plague them.

For instance, the shooting of Michael Brown in Ferguson, Missouri, brought out a litany of black church pastors and preachers to help quell the demonstrations and the open hostility between the citizenry and the police. In Baltimore, Maryland, Jamal Bryant, pastor of a church in the area, grabbed local and international headlines speaking out about the death of Freddie Gray at the hands of the Baltimore Police Department.

Where was the black church as a whole? Aside from pastoring in their respective communities, where was the National Baptist Convention? Where was their ever any type of consolidated effort from T. D. Jakes or any other pastor with funds and acclaim in the black church galvanizing efforts to come together on an international stage to stand up for the rights of people of color? Where were the devout pastors when their members or nonmembers were out fighting, picketing for fair treatment from law enforcement officials?

Since I brought up Jamal Bryant, I have to be fair to his involvement in Black Lives Matter. Reverend Jamal Bryant, lead pastor of Empowerment Temple AME Church in Baltimore, Maryland, brought three hundred pastors together to discuss the Black Lives movement in the aftermath of the senseless killing of Freddie Gray, allegedly at the hands of the Baltimore Police Department. In her article "Black Lives Matter is a black church matter,"[113] Najuma Smith-Pollard describes the gathering of these pastors, appointed "leaders" of their respective communities of color to "listen, learn and leave with strategies to build communities (of color)." Not surprising to me, the "strategies" discussed have been tossed around by pastors and pundits for as long

---

[113] Smith-Pollard, Najuma"Black Lives Matter.".

as I can remember; however, they never seem to get any mileage in the black community, or, if they do, they stall out.

The four major areas of emphasis were "Black Lives Matter, Black Dollars Matter, Black Minds Matter, and Black Votes Matter."[114] At the conclusion of the conference, which was held for four days, the strategies to be implemented were: social justice ministries within the local church, youth departments as conduits for activism, local school advocacy, narratives about HBCUs, and collective banking and bargaining.[115]

Now there has to be a dialogue, a plan has to be formed and collectively agreed upon, and then implemented. I really believe that this generation of black folks, post-civil-rights and desegregation, truly has nothing that galvanizes them to care collectively for each other to the extent that postslavery, Jim Crow, freedom riders, and KKK violence did for our predecessors. Quite frankly, the black church cannot and will not be able to nationally galvanize because the black church has let the very people it should protect down and has cast off any and all who don't conform to its beliefs, whether they be intrinsic within the individual church or as a Christian community.

Our values as individuals and as dictated by Christianity have become watered down and inclusive. We would rather not be pariahs

---

114 Ibid.

115 Ibid.

but be socially accepted by everyone. These days, to speak a point about Jesus or the teachings of Jesus can lead to banishment quicker than an atheist getting bounced out of a Sunday school class.

The black church has lost its way, and I don't think it seems to care past its own doorstep. In my opinion, the church only cares about its individual bottom line. The pastor with the biggest church and the biggest following *has* to be living right and following the word of God; therefore, we should follow him and join him and send him money and keep his ministry and building afloat and paid for.

I mentioned the murder of Michael Brown in Ferguson, Missouri, which was ground zero for the Black Lives Matter movement. Michelle Higgins is the director of worship and outreach at the St. Louis City Church in St. Louis, Missouri.

According to Ms. Higgins, in an interview she did with *Relevant Magazine*, "The Church became comfortable in just holding hands and singing. The Church became comfortable in putting all our happy times inside the sanctuary and beginning to ignore a wave of injustices outside the sanctuary walls. The Church has decided to protect for innocent victims instead of do a holistic cry for the sanctity of all life, those who are 'naughty' and those who are 'nice.' We missed our chance to be the Black Lives Movement. The church should embrace

Black Lives Matter because Black Lives Matter is preaching the gospel of life, hope and of justice better than we are."[116]

The black church is nothing more than a black tax-free business whose inclusion is determined by your ethnicity, your tithes and offerings, and your unquestioning loyalty and submission to your pastor, as allegedly appointed and affirmed by God.

The black church has indeed lost its prophetic voice, its own belief in itself, perhaps due to a lack of real leadership and a lack of individuals of color who believe in God more than they do themselves and the pastor.

Ms. Higgins also noted in her interview that those who were on the front lines of the Black Lives Matter movement were not members of any church. I don't know if she polled anyone or has any credible statistical evidence or is basing her statement on the clashes and property damage and violence of the days following the murder of Michael Brown, but she was a lot closer to the fires than I was.

The black church has relegated itself to money-making enterprise and sequestering itself. No sinner can gain admittance for fear that the church itself will be corrupted by his or her mere presence. The black church has to be willing to express itself not only in terms of its history but be willing to escape the paradigm of its past success (civil rights

---

[116] Ibid.

movement), and, through faith, vision, and sacrifice, take on the most common and morally corrosive issues of our time.

The Black Lives Matter movement, the genocide in Chicago, gun control laws, college tuition rate hikes, student loan debt, job creation, and small business growth in the black community are important issues. The black church that I know and envision and can get behind is an active social gospel and not just the continuation of a narrative long since spun and written.

When more church pastors, these self-appointed leaders, begin to lead within their spiritual confines, preaching the gospel to the nations and not merely their own members, and choose to accept labels such as leaders, and can show it on such a level that the community as a whole can get behind them, maybe, just maybe, the black church can live again. Until that time, the black church is just a word, a hype, a fleeting memory of more gallant and powerful times whose nostalgia is just enough to keep people attending and tithing and praise dancing and singing and partying within the four walls of the building they attend every Sunday with the promise that when they die, the pastor will preach at their funeral and say good words about them, and that God will reward their faithfulness to their church.

By the way, as luck would have it, another session is scheduled for September 2016 with Kansas City, Missouri, as the host city yet again. I hope this time I can attend and discover what the function of the convention is and what the convention is offering to the public at large.

I don't know what citywide changes, if any, transpired between the last meeting and the upcoming meeting, but there have been a rash of murders and crimes afflicting Kansas City, Missouri. People are still dying, and as far as I can discern, there have been no new interfaith ministries between the black church and any of its counterparts in this area, at least none advertised.

As I went online to discover what the purpose or the aims of the convention were, I saw the pictures of pastors and their titles, some claiming doctoral degrees, who were on a committee for planning, and pictures of the Kansas City Royals baseball team, a picture of the Kansas City skyline, and pictures of various Kansas City, Missouri, businesses and even a tab for "Visit KC." I assume this was a vacation from all of the ministry and work the individual churches had been doing in their respective communities. Strange how this page only mentioned a quote from the Bible about a conqueror.

What has the black church conquered since the civil rights movement? It appears that the "black church" is now similar to the same Christianity that birthed it: separate and segregated, bent to the desires and whims of a pastor who was called by a God no one has ever seen to do a work in the community in which they all separately live.

It reminds me of the Saturday morning cartoon *The Super Friends*—Superman, Batman, Aquaman, and Wonder Woman, you know the rest. Each of the members has individual strengths and weaknesses. However, they banded together to take on threats that none could handle separately. Each weakness would be countered by the strength of another teammate. The goal of the team is to fight for truth and justice.

Each individual black church open in the name of Christ has a particular strength and/or weakness due to size, the cult of personality of the pastor, the financial standing of the members, the rate of giving among the members, and the faithfulness of each member of the church toward the pastors' dictates. You get what I mean.

For example, Aquaman's strength lies in his primary domain: the oceans. He has telepathic power over all the life in the sea, and he can swim very fast underwater. The ocean is where his strength lies.

However, you take him out of the ocean, and he is nearly powerless. His heart is in the right place, but he cannot live up to his true strength and prowess unless he is in his *element.*

What element is *your* church in? Where is your church functioning that shows its peak of holy power? Is it big business? Finance? Evangelism? Feeding the poor and the homeless? Music workshops? Sunday morning worship workers? (These include ushers, musicians, deacons, audio/visual ministry, "counselors," new members' orientation classes, and teachers, all of the necessary elements that structure a typical Sunday morning worship at your church.) Most of you, I believe, would say your church's focus is primarily raising money and increasing membership.

If the black church wants to be alive and relevant and powerful again, it must change with the times. I did not say compromise. I said change with the times. The civil rights movement did not only include blacks, so the black church cannot grow and proper without the acknowledgment and inclusion of others in the struggle for humanity and as US citizens.

The black church should stand as a beacon that envelops not only black people in this new paradigm but shows common ground among all of humanity. By sharing ideals and principles, perhaps the solutions the black church and the black community are searching for, hungering for, can be resolved by gathering information from without, and then transporting them within.

Note: At the time of this writing, I had attempted to gain permission from the National Baptist Convention to shoot a documentary for research purposes of a planned second book.

However, even though I submitted my documentation and provided information to the Media Relations Department, I was told that the board still had questions about my purpose for wanting to shoot a documentary and wanted to meet me in Kansas City. I was electronically provided a location and a time but not a meeting site.

I was not contacted again until nearly ten minutes *after* the meeting in Kansas City had begun on September 5 with the location of the meeting. I called the contact person and was told that not only did I have to personally answer questions from the board, but my filming had to be put to yet another vote on the day the convention was to begin in Kansas City.

Why the blatant attempt to ignore me? Why is the convention so protective of its session? Why the late notice to meet the day of the first night of the convention with no guarantees of approval?

My request was benign, and I had planned to only capture what was present at the convention, and was prepared to have releases passed out and signed by all those who freely chose to engage and participate.

I figured that I was not going to get permission because the National Baptist Convention USA is very protective of its mission. I was not too disappointed because I had prepared myself for it. At any rate, I left the National Baptist Convention with the same piece of advice I received from a pastor who contacted me about the survey I sent to his church and directed me to Acts chapter 5. I won't quote the entire passage, but to summarize the events that transpired, the apostles were being persecuted by the high priests and the Sadducees for performing miracles among the people in Jerusalem, making believers of them along the way.[117]

The high priest and his crew, jealous, initially jailed Peter and his

---

[117] Acts 5:12–18 (KJV).

fellows for their actions instead of killing them outright, lest they make the citizenry upset.[118]

The disciples were freed from their temporary imprisonment by an angel and were directed to continue declaring the Good News. They were caught again by the high priest and his crew and then brought before the Sanhedrin for continuing to teach in Jesus's name.[119]

The apostles, during the hearing, professed their belief in Jesus and said they were commissioned by the Holy Spirit to continue to serve the people and proclaim the tale of Jesus's continuing mission.[120] However, a law school teacher named Gamaliel stood up in the Sanhedrin and, in privately addressing the Sanhedrin, said that due to past experience with these types of people, they should leave the apostles to their own devices.[121]

What comes next is the part of this passage that is applicable to all churches that supposedly are open in the name of Jesus, declaring the Good News and serving the community, and with my efforts to get Christians to become believers and get out of their own way and allow God to do what God will.

Gamaliel states, "If their purpose or activity is of human origin, it

---

118 Acts 5:18 (KJV).

119 Ibid., 19–27.

120 Ibid., 29.

121 Ibid., 38.

will fail. But if it is from God, you will not be able to stop these men; you will only find yourselves fighting against God."

I know that riches and fame and notoriety can be construed as blessings from God, and those observing these Christians assume that they are doing the right thing. However, it's time for the black church to admit to what it has become or what it is not and salvage itself to remain relevant in the twenty-first century if black America, and all of America, is going to meet the challenges our nation and our world continue to face.

BIBLIOGRAPHY

Holy Bible, King James and New King James Versions.

Glaude, Eddie. "The Black Church Is Dead." *Huffington Post*, February 24, 2010.

Aslan, Resa. *The Life and Times of Jesus of Nazareth*. Random House. New York 2013.

The Voting Rights Act of 1965.

Hayes, Terry. *I Am Pilgrim*. SimonandSchuster. London. 2012.

Bradley, Jonathan. *Liberating Black Theology*. Crossway Books. Wheaton, IL 2010.

Evans, Curtis. *The Burden of Black Religion*. Oxford University Press. New York. 2008.

Delaney, Martin. *The Condition, Elevation, Emigration and Destiny of the Colored People of the United States.*

Obergefell v. Hodges, Director, Ohio Department of Health, 576 U.S. 201, 135 S.Ct. 2584 (2014).

Brown v. Board of Education of Topeka, Kansas et al. 347 U.S. 483 (1954).

United States Tax Code section 501.

US Constitution, Amend. 1, Sec. 1.

"Six Facts about Black Americans for Black History Month," Pew Research Center (2015).

Journal of Blacks in Higher Education. www.jbhe.com News and Views Statistics 2009.

PEW Forum on Religion and Public Life, 2009.

Dixon, James II. *If God Is So Good, Why Are Blacks Doing So Bad.* Lifebridge Books, Charlotte, NC 2007.

Burrell, Tom. *Brainwashed: Challenging the Myth of Black Inferiority.* Smileybooks, New York, NY 2011.

Washington, Booker T. *Up from Slavery: An Autobiography*. Doubleday, Page & Co., New York, 1907.

Luther, Martin. *The Freedom of a Christian*. Fortress Press, Minneapolis 2008.

Smith-Pollard, Najuma. "Black Lives Matter is a black church matter." Center for Religion and Civil Culture, March 9, 2016.

Hansbury, Aaron Cline. "Why the Church Should Support Black Lives Matter." *Relevant Magazine*, January 16, 2016.

Printed in the United States
By Bookmasters